Rhetoric for Today

FOURTH EDITION

Rhetoric for Today

FOURTH EDITION

William F. Smith
FULLERTON COLLEGE

Raymond D. Liedlich
CONTRA COSTA COLLEGE

HARCOURT BRACE JOVANOVICH, INC.

New York   Chicago   San Francisco   Atlanta

Cover photograph by Glen Heller

ISBN: 0-15-577052-7

Library of Congress Catalog Card Number: 76-51933

Printed in the United States of America

Preface

Rhetoric for Today is intended to help students express their thoughts and opinions clearly and persuasively. It emphasizes basic rhetorical principles, beginning with the paragraph and concluding with the complete theme. It concentrates primarily on exposition and argumentation, the forms of writing most essential for success in college and most frequently used thereafter.

The Fourth Edition follows the pattern of its predecessors. The first three chapters provide explicit, detailed discussions of unity, development, and coherence as those elements relate to the expository paragraph. Chapter Four introduces in clear and simple terms the fundamentals of sound thinking and shows students how to apply them to the writing process. This chapter has been expanded to give a more complete explanation and illustration of inductive and deductive thinking. Chapter Five presents step-by-step instruction for writing the complete theme; it also includes a short discussion of another fundamental rhetorical principle: emphasis. Each chapter ends with a brief review of the main topics covered; Chapter Five contains a final summary of important points from the first three chapters as well as a checklist of steps essential to preparing the complete theme.

More than seventy sample paragraphs (one-third are new to this edition) illustrate each rhetorical principle as it is presented. Most of these paragraphs have enough intrinsic interest and are sufficiently self-contained to afford opportunity for discussion and writing. In addition to the illustrative paragraphs, more than seventy-five exercises on tear-out sheets encourage immediate application of the lessons as they are studied; most have been revised to include new material. A careful reading of the text and a conscientious working of the exercises should lead students, through both precept and practice, to shape the raw materials of their own experience into clear, meaningful units of expository or argumentative prose.

We appreciate the many helpful suggestions given us by the members of the English Departments at Fullerton College, Portland Community College, De Anza College, and Contra Costa College, as well as the encouragement and support of our wives, Dorothy and Martha.

W.F.S.
R.D.L.

Contents

CHAPTER FIVE   The Theme   175

Rhetoric for Today

FOURTH EDITION

CHAPTER ONE | Unity

An essential quality of all good writing is *unity,* or singleness of purpose. The paragraph is a unit of thought concerned with the exposition of a single idea, and if it is to communicate that idea clearly and concisely, it must possess oneness. That is, all the detail — the reasons, illustrations, facts — used to develop it must pertain to one controlling idea. Consider, for example, the following paragraph:

> One of the generalities most often noted about Americans is that we are a restless, a dissatisfied, a searching people. We bridle and buck under failure, and we go mad with dissatisfaction in the face of success. We spend our time searching for security, and hate it when we get it. For the most part we are an intemperate people: we eat too much when we can, drink too much, indulge our senses too much. Even in our so-called virtues we are intemperate: a teetotaler is not content not to drink — he must stop all the drinking in the world; a vegetarian among us would outlaw the eating of meat. We work too hard, and many die under the strain; and then to make up for that we play with a violence as suicidal. [From John Steinbeck, "Paradox and Dream," from *America and Americans,* The Viking Press, 1966.]

The controlling idea of this paragraph is contained in the first sentence, "One of the generalities most often noted about Americans is that we are a restless, a dissatisfied, a searching people," and the following sentences provide supporting detail. To illustrate his point, Steinbeck mentions several American traits. Americans fear failure, but are bored with success. They eat and drink too much, but the vegetarian wants to outlaw meat eating and the teetotaler the drinking of alcohol. To compensate for the strain of hard work, which kills many, they resort to play that is similarly destructive.

3

THE TOPIC SENTENCE

The sentence that expresses the controlling idea of a paragraph is called the *topic sentence*. In the paragraph above, it is the first sentence, the sentence on which the unity of the paragraph is based. An important first step in achieving paragraph unity is to express your thought in a topic sentence and place that sentence at the beginning of your paragraph. A beginning topic sentence provides an organizational focus, a guideline that will help you to stick to your subject. It will not guarantee paragraph unity, however. The following paragraph, for example, begins with a topic sentence, but it does not prevent the writer from wandering off the subject.

Evaluating college teachers is not a simple matter. The most common approach employed by colleges and universities today is to ask the student. Student evaluation of the faculty appeals to college administrators because it is simple, convenient, and, most important, popular with students. But it is not foolproof. Since tough, demanding teachers tend to get lower marks on student evaluation cards and student evaluation has been given serious consideration in faculty promotions, a significant number of teachers have reacted by lowering course requirements and by giving a much higher percentage of A's and B's. Of course, tough teachers are not invariably good teachers. In fact, too many who preach high standards simply lack the patience, perseverance, and enthusiasm that good teaching demands. And finally, student evaluation has diverted teacher attention from the difficult but important task of stimulating student interest in ideas and the life of the mind to theatrics, to developing a popular personality in the classroom.

In the first five sentences of this paragraph, the writer stays on the subject. The first sentence presents the main point, and the second introduces a currently popular method of faculty evaluation—asking students to rate their teachers. The third sentence supports the second sentence by explaining why administrators favor student evaluation, and the fourth and fifth sentences explain the weakness in such evaluation. But the sixth and seventh sentences stray from the controlling idea. From a consideration of the disadvantages of faculty evaluation by students, the writer turns to a peripheral issue, whether tough teachers are good teachers. The last sentence returns to the main point: student evaluation of faculty often diverts a teacher's attention from the most important task of stimulating student interest in ideas to theatrics.

What has happened in this paragraph often happens in students' paragraphs. Although students place the topic sentence first and use it as a guide for supporting sentences, they may nevertheless insert irrelevant ideas. Why? One important reason is that they have not focused sharply enough on a controlling idea in the topic sentence. The topic sentence of the paragraph above seemed sufficiently broad to the writer to justify the comments on the relation between advocating high standards and a lack of patience, perseverence, and enthusiasm on the part of tough, demanding teachers. Had the writer narrowed the topic in his topic sentence and stressed a controlling idea, he would have been less likely to introduce extraneous ideas into the paragraph. Consider this revised version:

> Evaluating college teachers is not a simple matter because of the difficulty in developing sound, acceptable measuring devices. The most common approach employed by colleges and universities today is to ask the student. Student evaluation of the faculty appeals to college administrators because it is simple, convenient, and, most important, popular with students. But it is not foolproof. Since tough, demanding teachers tend to get lower marks on student evaluation cards and student evaluation has been given serious consideration in faculty promotions, a significant number of teachers have reacted by lowering course requirements and by giving a much higher percentage of A's and B's. Another way to evaluate teaching skill is to test student learning on objective tests—the more information mastered in a unit of time, the better the teacher. But this approach also has undesirable consequences. It forces teachers to teach to the test, to force-feed students to score higher on the test and thereby produce higher marks for their teacher. This approach also stresses learning for the moment, factual regurgitation. It overlooks the fact that real learning takes time for reflection, for thoughtful digestion. And, finally, objective measurements do not require students to integrate, organize, and apply what has been learned. College administrators agree that objective tests and student ratings to measure teaching skill are not perfect, but they argue that they are better than nothing. Critics of these devices, however, argue that whatever good they produce is offset by their harmful effect on the curriculum and teaching practice.

The topic sentence of this revised version is more pointed. To the original topic sentence, "Evaluating college teachers is not a simple matter," the phrase "because of the difficulty in developing sound, acceptable measuring devices" has been added. This new topic sentence stresses a controlling idea. It signals reader and writer alike that the paragraph will discuss why, in terms of the harmful effects of current, widely used devices for testing teacher effectiveness, evaluating college teachers is not a simple matter. The writer has now more tightly defined the subject, and is therefore less likely to be tempted to introduce irrelevant matter.

THE CONTROLLING IDEA

Make certain, then, that your topic sentence contains a key word or group of words that expresses a controlling idea. Occasionally the entire topic sentence will be needed to express this idea, but more frequently it will be expressed in a word or phrase. A controlling idea will help you to limit your subject to one that you can deal with more completely in a paragraph and to avoid the kind of broad, general topic sentence that tempts students to include a variety of detail only loosely related to their central idea. Here are some examples of broad, general topic sentences with suggested revisions of them. Each revision sharpens the focus of the original sentence by stressing a controlling idea.

ORIGINAL	REVISED
To the Moon by J. Chapman is an interesting book.	*To the Moon* by J. Chapman presents an interesting account of the problems of landing a man on the moon.
Professional ice hockey is exciting.	Professional ice hockey is fiercely competitive.
Communism is evil.	Communism threatens man's individuality by restricting his freedom of expression.
Theodore Roosevelt was a good president.	Theodore Roosevelt did much to preserve the natural beauty of America.

The topic sentence of a paragraph may include more than one idea, as in the following sentence:

The study of psychology is *interesting* and *useful*.

The two ideas in this topic sentence could be developed, although briefly of course, in a single paragraph. The controlling idea in this next sentence, however, is too comprehensive for development in one paragraph:

.America is a *democratic society* based on a system of *free enterprise,* which emphasizes *individual initiative.*

Adequate development of the ideas in this sentence would require several paragraphs, for each of the italicized terms would have to be explained and illustrated. To attempt such a discussion in a single paragraph would create serious problems in unity, especially for an inexperienced writer.

EXERCISE 1

Underline the topic sentence and circle the controlling idea in the following paragraphs.

1. The primitive confusion of word with thing, of symbol with thing symbolized, manifests itself in some parts of the world in a belief that the name of a person is *part* of that person. To know someone's name, therefore, is to have power over him. Because of this belief, it is customary among some peoples for children to be given at birth a "real name" known only to the parents and never used, as well as a nickname or public name to be called by in society. In this way the child is protected from being put in someone's power. The story of Rumpelstilskin is a European illustration of this belief in the power of names. [From *Language in Thought and Action*, Third Edition, S. I. Hayakawa. Page 67. Harcourt Brace Jovanovich, Inc.]

2. The processes of creative activity display several striking features. One of the most frequent is the occurrence of flashes of insight outside the hours of regular work, during periods of physical activity or at odd moments of reverie or relaxation when the mind is daydreaming. Poincaré tells how the further steps of his discovery of the Fuchsian functions came to him, with a sense of absolute certainty, "just as I put my foot on the step (of a wagonette), and again, "as I was crossing the street." Similar examples are endless, and give comforting glimpses of the ordinary daily life of genius. Mozart got the idea for the melody of the "Magic Flute" quintet while playing billiards, Berlioz found himself humming a musical phrase he had long sought in vain as he rose from a dive while bathing in the Tiber, Sir William Hamilton, a great mathematical physicist, thought of quarternions (a new mathematical method) while strolling with his wife in the streets of Dublin, and the chemist Kekule saw the atoms dancing in midair and so conceived his theory of atomic groupings while riding on the top of a London bus. [From Lancelot Law Whyte, "Where Do Those Bright Ideas Come From?" *Harper's Magazine*, © 1951 Harper & Brothers, Inc. Reprinted by permission of A. Watkins, Inc.]

3. Still, the status of the assembly line has been declining for some time now; other reasons must explain why the protest has only surfaced in the last couple of years. First, younger men are an ever more important part of the world force; 40 percent of the current UAW members are under thirty. Second, some are increasingly unhappy with the union, which is more responsive to older workers—and *they* are naturally more interested in pensions than working conditions. Also, as B. J. Widick wrote recently in the *Nation,* "The old-timers think of the UAW as an organization that protects them from company abuse. Young workers think of the UAW as an outfit that had better get them what they think they deserve, and now. The young are not burdened with memories of the miseries of the past or the struggles of two decades ago." A third factor is the current recession. During more affluent years, dissatisfied assembly line workers could find better jobs outside the factory; now, these jobs are scarcer and the men feel trapped on the

line. [From Herbert J. Gans, "The Protest of Young Factory Workers," *New Generation*, Fall, 1970. Reprinted by permission of The National Child Labor Committee.]

4. Grown-up life is, still, a life of ruthless competition where promotion depends on the equivalent of marks. And these are accorded by business, industry and the professions — publicly and without the slightest consideration of potential trauma. The man who makes it to a corporation presidency is *never* one who was sheltered from competition and spared the spiritual blow of constant comparative rating with his associates. Nor was he a man who went up the ladder with what would have been a D-minus grade at every rung. In sum, education by the philosophy now inbred into teaching is utterly unsuitable as preparation for real life in a real world because it is, basically *nothing education*. [From Philip Wylie, "Generation of Zeros," reprinted by permission of Harold Ober Associates Incorporated. Copyright © 1967 by Philip Wylie.]

5. Man is but a reed, the weakest thing in nature, but he is a reed that thinks. It is not necessary that the whole universe should arm itself to crush him. A vapor, a drop of water, is enough to kill him. But if the universe should crush him, man would still be nobler than that which slays him, for he knows that he dies; but of the advantage which it has over him the universe knows nothing. Our dignity consists, then, wholly in thought. Our elevation must come from this, not from space and time, which we cannot fill. Let us, then, labor to think well: this is the fundamental principle of morals. [From Blaise Pascal, *Pensées*.]

EXERCISE 2

A. The controlling idea of a topic sentence is the key word or group of words that expresses its basic idea. In the following topic sentences circle the word or words that contain the controlling idea.

EXAMPLE   A dictionary is a(useful)book for a college student.

1. At least three easily distinguishable kinds of college professors can be found on American campuses today.

2. The practice of civil disobedience to effect political and social changes involves serious consequences both for the practitioner and the larger society.

3. Young people can be of great help to a political campaigner.

4. Good English is clear, appropriate, and vivid.

5. Filling out a federal income tax form is a bewildering and frustrating experience.

6. Richard Wagner, the great composer, was in many ways an unscrupulous man.

7. The modern whaling ship is more elaborate than its predecessor in the nineteenth century.

8. Sociologists point to a number of causes for student protest in the 1960s.

9. The value of a person in contemporary America is frequently a matter of economic rather than moral considerations.

10. The word *classic* has a variety of meanings.

B. Revise the following topic sentences to narrow the focus and stress a dominant idea.

EXAMPLE

ORIGINAL   The new Phaeton automobile is a fine car.
REVISION   Superior workmanship, beautiful design, and economic operation make the new Phaeton a fine automobile.

1. Some students have an easy time in college.

_____

_____

2. The proposal to abolish traditional marriage ties for a short-term renewable contract is intriguing.

_____

_____

3. Advertising often has a bad influence on people.

_____

_____

4. A primary cause for the so-called generation gap in many families is a teen-ager's language.

_____

_____

5. Foreign travel is good for Americans.

_____

_____

6. If the American economy is to continue to function well, both labor and management will have to be controlled.

_____

_____

7. The new X-109 Martin roadster is a fantastic car.

_____

_____

8. Governmental attempts to force journalists to reveal their sources should be resisted.

_____

_____

9. Professor Daugherty's latest book, _Inside Australia's Outback,_ is an interesting study.

_____

_____

10. The transportation system in this country will have to be redesigned.

_____

_____

PRIMARY AND SECONDARY
SUPPORTING DETAIL

When your topic sentence is somewhat complicated, you will often have to develop your paragraph more extensively than when your topic sentence is simple. In this case, some of your sentences will contain more important ideas than others. That is, the detail in some sentences will directly support the controlling idea, whereas the detail in other sentences will explain and clarify these direct supporting statements. We can thus conveniently distinguish between *primary* support—detail that relates directly to the main idea of the paragraph —and *secondary* support—detail that explains and clarifies primary support. In the following paragraph the topic idea is supported by a number of primary statements, each of which relates directly to the controlling idea of the topic sentence—the benefits to wild animals of forest fires.

Countless animals and plants rely upon fire to maintain habitats in a healthy state. Deer rest and feed in the open spaces cleared by fire in and around forests. Elk once wintered in valleys kept clear by fire. Many shore birds, waterfowl, and songbirds need treeless spaces to feed and nest; cattail marshes, if unburned, become impenetrable for the herons and rails that live there. Muskrat catches in the productive areas of Louisiana and Maryland fell dramatically after Smokey the Bear prevented the trappers' customary burning of decadent vegetation after each season. Woodcocks and quail cannot forage on a forest floor that accumulates more than about six inches of litter, and their numbers are dropping in fire-free areas. [From Richard J. Vogl, "Smokey's Mid-Career Crisis." Copyright 1973 by Saturday Review Co. First appeared in *Saturday Review*, March 1973, p. 27. Used with permission.]

In this next paragraph the topic sentence is supported by two primary statements and three secondary statements.

I have come to marvel at the instinct of animals to make use of natural laws for healing themselves. They know unerringly which herbs will cure what ills. Wild creatures first seek solitude and absolute relaxation, then they rely on the complete remedies of Nature—the medicine in plants and pure air. A bear grubbing for fern roots; a wild turkey compelling her babies in a rainy spell to eat leaves of the spice bush; an animal, bitten by a poisonous snake, confidently chewing snakeroot—all these are typical examples. An animal with fever quickly hunts up an airy, shady place near water, there remaining quiet, eating nothing but drinking often until its health is recovered. On the other hand, an animal bedeviled by rheumatism finds a spot of hot sunlight and lies in it until the misery bakes out. [From D. C. Jarvis, *Folk Medicine*, p. 10. Holt, Rinehart and Winston, Inc.]

An analysis of each of these two paragraphs illuminates this difference between primary and secondary supporting statements.

CONTROLLING IDEA

Countless animals and plants rely upon fire to maintain habitats in a healthy state.

Primary Support
1. Deer rest and feed in spaces cleared by fire.
2. Elk spent the winters in valleys kept clear by fire.
3. Birds need treeless spaces to feed and nest and herons and rails need to be able to penetrate cattail marshes for a living place.
4. The muskrat population in Louisiana and Maryland declined because fire had not burned off decadent vegetation.
5. Woodcocks and quail need [clean] forest floors [floors that are] kept clean of litter by fire.

CONTROLLING IDEA

Animals have an instinct for using natural laws to heal themselves.

Primary Support
1. Animals know unerringly which herbs will cure what ills.
2. They first seek solitude and absolute relaxation and then rely on natural remedies—the medicine in plants and pure air.

Secondary Support

A bear grubbing for fern roots; a wild turkey compelling her babies in a rainy spell to eat leaves of the spice bush; an animal, bitten by a poisonous snake, chewing snakeroot—all are typical examples.

An animal with fever quickly hunts up an airy, shady place near water where it remains quiet, eating nothing but drinking often until its health is recovered.

An animal troubled by rheumatism lies in hot sunlight to bake out its misery.

When you have decided on a topic sentence, then, examine its controlling idea carefully. If it is fairly complex, you will probably need both primary and secondary support to develop it adequately. The writer of the following paragraph uses both primary and secondary support to develop the controlling idea.

The men who rush into undertakings of vast change usually feel they are in possession of some irresistible power. The generation that made the French Revolution had an extravagant conception of the omnipotence of man's reason and the boundless range of his intelligence. Never, says de Tocqueville, had humanity been prouder of itself nor had it ever so much faith in its own omnipotence. And joined with this exaggereated self-confidence was a universal thirst for change which came unbidden to every mind. Lenin and the Bolsheviks who plunged recklessly into the chaos of the creation of a new world had blind faith in the omnipotence of Marxist doctrine. The Nazis had nothing as potent as that doctrine, but they had faith in an infallible leader and also faith in a new technique. For it is doubtful whether National Socialism would have made such rapid progress if it had not been for the electrifying conviction that the new techniques of blitzkrieg and propaganda made Germany irresistible. [From p. 8 in *The True Believer* by Eric Hoffer. Copyright, 1951 by Eric Hoffer. Reprinted by permission of Harper & Row, Publishers, Inc.]

The controlling idea of this paragraph is contained in the first sentence: "The men who rush into undertakings of vast change usually feel they are in possession of some irresistible power." Three primary supporting statements are used to support the controlling idea. What are they? Which sentences provide illustration and clarification of these primary statements? A clear understanding of the way this paragraph is assembled should provide practical guidance when you find you have to supply more than primary support to develop an idea in a paragraph.

This discussion of primary and secondary detail is intended to clarify a basic characteristic of the structure of the expository or argumentative paragraph. As you will discover in your reading and writing, however, this distinction is not precisely applicable to every paragraph of this type. Every sentence of such a paragraph does not necessarily add a new primary or secondary supporting detail. Some sentences, particularly those at the beginning of a paragraph that is part of a longer composition, may refer to an idea developed in a preceding paragraph. Other sentences may simply repeat, as a means of emphasis, an idea in a preceding sentence of the same paragraph.

In the following excerpt from T. S. Matthews' "What Makes News," for example, the first three sentences of the second paragraph deal with one idea—the putative power of the press to influence public opinion. The first sentence, "In what way is the press supposed to be so powerful?" iterates the thought of the topic sentence of the preceding paragraph and thus serves to link these two paragraphs together. The next sentence, "The general notion is that the press can form, control, or at least strongly influence opinion," expands upon the idea of the preceding sentence by elucidating the "way" in which the press is thought to exert its power. And the third sentence, "Can it really do any of these things?" contains the controlling idea that the following sentences develop.

Topic
Sentence

The biggest piece of claptrap about the press is that it deals exclusively, or even mainly, with news. *And the next biggest piece of claptrap is that the press has enormous power.* This delusion is persistent and widespread. It is taken for granted by the public-at-large, who are apt to be impressed by anything that is said three times; it is continually advertised by the press itself; and it is cherished by press lords, some of whom, at least, should know better.

Linking
Sentence

Topic
Sentence

(1) In what way is the press supposed to be so powerful? (2) The general notion is that the press can form, control, or at least strongly influence public opinion. (3) *Can it really do any of these things?* Hugh Cudlipp, editorial director of the London *Daily Mirror,* and a man who should know something about the effect of newspapers on public opinion, doesn't share this general notion about their power. He thinks newspapers can echo and stimulate a wave of popular feeling, but that's all: "A newspaper may successfully accelerate but never reverse the popular attitude, which common sense has commended to the public." In short, it can jump aboard the bandwagon, once the bandwagon is under way, but it can't start the bandwagon rolling or change its direction once it has started. [From T. S. Matthews, "What Makes News," *The Atlantic Monthly,* December, 1957, p. 82. Copyright © 1957 by T. S. Matthews. Reprinted by permission of the author.]

EXERCISE 3

A. In the following exercise a topic sentence and three sentences containing primary support are supplied as material for a paragraph. Supply the necessary secondary support in the blanks provided.

TOPIC SENTENCE   Students who work their way through college gain several benefits.

Primary Support
1. They gain valuable work experience.

   Secondary Support

   a. _____

   _____

   b. _____

   _____

Primary Support
2. They learn how to manage money.

   Secondary Support

   a. _____

   _____

   b. _____

   _____

Primary Support
3. But most important, they develop and strengthen character traits that will serve them well throughout their adult lives.

   Secondary Support

   a. _____

   _____

   b. _____

   _____

B. Read the following paragraph carefully and analyze it, following the examples of paragraph analysis presented on page 14. That is, write out its controlling idea and the primary and secondary supporting sentences.

Families who like to go camping can now choose from a variety of recreation vehicles, each one designed to meet a specific need. For the family that regularly takes long vacations every summer, in addition to monthly treks to the mountains or seashore, and wants a good deal of comfort and convenience, the motor home is a good choice. Prices range from approximately $10,000 to $45,000—the higher the cost, the greater the luxury. The basic advantage of the motor home is that it is self-contained and comfortable. All the fuss and inconvenience usually connected with setting up and taking down camping gear is eliminated. Families that take an occasional outing in the woods on a weekend, of course, would not need the fancy motor home. For them the converted van or the pickup camper would suffice. Like the motor home, the van provides self-contained eating and sleeping—but not bathing—facilities. It would, however, be a bit crowded for a large family. The pickup camper has similar facilities, but it is usually roomier. And the smaller size camper, because it has a more durable suspension system, is more suitable for rough terrain. The camper-trailer opens up to form a tent-like covering for shelter. It fits the needs of hardy campers, those who do not demand so much comfort but who want more than a ground-level tent between them and the elements. The variety of recreation vehicles now available makes it possible for most camping families to choose a vehicle that fits their camping needs and their budget.

CONTROLLING IDEA _____

_____

Primary Support and *Secondary Support*

_____

_____

_____

_____

_____

_____

PLACEMENT OF THE TOPIC SENTENCE

We have suggested that you place the topic sentence first. This advice is especially valid for inexperienced writers, for a beginning topic sentence provides the best guideline and the most effective check against irrelevant matter. However, as you gain skill and experience in writing lucid, well-developed paragraphs, you may occasionally wish to place the topic sentence elsewhere. For example, you may use it not to announce your controlling idea but to reinforce it at the conclusion of your paragraph. Presenting your evidence first lets your readers see the reasoning that supports your idea, in which case they are more apt to accept it than they would if it were presented at the beginning of your paragraph. In the following paragraph the topic sentence appears at the end of the paragraph.

Within the past thirty years, Americans have become increasingly more mobile, increasingly more addicted to moving around. According to a recent study, an American family changes its residence on the average of once every five years. Approximately forty million Americans change their address every year. The number of Americans living in mobile homes has also grown dramatically. Each year more and more people are lured by the prospect of being able to move their homes to other neighborhoods, cities, or states with a minimum of fuss. The effect of this heavy internal migration, however, has been to disrupt and uproot family life and to make personal loyalties and commitments to community organizations and affairs more tenuous. Frequent movement breeds anonymity and indifference to others. It increases personal isolation and loss of identity. Some observers, in fact, attribute the increase in crime, divorce rates, alcoholism, drug addiction, loss of interest in local politics and community affairs, and a general voter disenchantment with and distrust of political and social institutions to the loss of personal and community contacts caused by this shifting population. American mobility, consequently, needs to be reexamined. By contributing to an alienation and weakening of social values, it is creating a serious problem for the health and stability of American life.

Another method is to begin and close with a topic sentence.

Clearly, there is no need of bringing on wars in order to breed heroes. Civilized life affords plenty of opportunities for heroes, and for a better kind than war or any other savagery has ever produced. Moreover, none but lunatics would set a city on fire in order to give opportunities for heroism to firemen, or introduce the cholera or yellow fever to give physicians and nurses opportunities for practicing disinterested devotion, or condemn thousands of people to extreme poverty in order that some well-to-do persons might practice a beautiful charity. It is equally crazy to advocate war on the ground that it is a school for heroes. [From Charles W. Eliot, "Five American Contributions to Civilization," *The Oxford Book of American Essays,* ed. Brander Mathews, The Century Company, 1914.]

In some paragraphs you may need two sentences to express your central idea. In the following paragraph the first two sentences convey the main idea, that memorizing rules of punctuation will not automatically ensure good writing.

Many rules have been formulated for the use of the various marks of punctuation, and people have thought that by simply memorizing these rules they might find a key to good writing. Unfortunately, as teachers of punctuation will be among the first to point out, this is not the case. By acting as a visual aid, punctuation can help one to comprehend a carefully thought piece of writing, but it cannot supply meaning. If a written composition, be it a letter, set of directions, or a critical essay, seems to lack precision and directness, the writer will do well to consider first of all whether it is properly organized, not whether it is properly punctuated. Ordinarily, meaningful and well-organized writing is not hard to punctuate. One's style of punctuation is generally determined by the type and purpose of the writing. Compared to a sports story in the daily paper, a treatise on physics will be marked by more complex constructions, and, accordingly, a greater amount of punctuation. This does not mean that one kind or style of punctuation is better than another. It simply indicates that the precise distinctions in thought and meaning which concern the scholar and scientist require more detailed, complex statement, and hence more detailed and complex punctuation, than the factual, comparatively simple story of a baseball game. The former type of writing is designed to compress a maximum amount of exact and complicated information within a limited space. The purpose of the latter is to provide a simple, easily readable account which will entertain and inform its readers. In both instances, the punctuation has the same function: to aid the writer in conveying his particular message to his readers. Punctuation that performs this function is "good" punctuation; when punctuation fails to realize this aim it is faulty. [From the *Thorndike-Barnhart Comprehensive Desk Dictionary* by E. L. Thorndike and Clarence L. Barnhart. Copyright © 1965 by Scott, Foresman and Company. Reprinted by permission of the publisher.]

The topic sentence of this next paragraph is the fourth sentence, "But this does not go down to the roots of American society. . . ." The first three sentences lead into this sentence, and the sentences following it develop its controlling idea, the masculine nature of American society.

During the last 50 years American women, chiefly through inheritance, have come to possess a formidable amount of economic power. This is a country of rich widows. The extent of their influence has helped to create this legend that women are in charge. But this does not go down to the roots of American society, does not change its fundamental character: It is still dominated by the masculine and not the feminine principle. How do I know? Well, here is a quite simple test. At the present time America possesses sufficient instruments of destruction to kill every man, woman and child on earth. This macabre achievement, which has demanded an astonishing amount of technical skill and superb organization and the expenditure of billions and billions of dollars, not only represents the masculine principle triumphantly asserting itself but also suggests the male mind coming to the end of its tether. Where is the feminine principle, where is Woman, in this madness? Where is the feminine emphasis here upon love, on the happiness of persons? Is this how women want their money spent? We have only to ask the question to know the answer. Here is a society shaped and colored by male values. It is about as much like a matriarchy as the Marine Corps. [From J. B. Priestley, "Women Don't Run the Country," *The Saturday Evening Post,* December 12, 1964. Reprinted with permission from *The Saturday Evening Post* © 1964 The Curtis Publishing Company.]

In some paragraphs, particularly narrative and descriptive paragraphs, the topic idea may be implied rather than explicitly stated. The implied topic idea of the paragraph below is a description of a Hindu prisoner, who is being taken from his cell to be hanged. Notice how carefully George Orwell selects his details to render a unified impression of the scene.

One prisoner had been brought out of his cell. He was a Hindu, a puny wisp of a man, with a shaven head and vague liquid eyes. He had a thick sprouting moustache, absurdly too big for his body, rather like the moustache of a comic man on the films. Six tall Indian warders were guarding him and getting him ready for the gallows. Two of them stood by with rifles and fixed bayonets, while the others handcuffed him, passed a chain through his handcuffs and fixed it to their belts, and lashed his arms tight to his sides. They crowded very close about him, with their hands always on him in a careful, caressing grip, as though all the while feeling him to make sure he was there. It was like men handling a fish which is still alive and may jump back into the water. But he stood quite unresisting, yielding his arms limply to the ropes, as though he hardly noticed what was happening. [From George Orwell, *Shooting An Elephant And Other Essays*, copyright, 1945, 1946, 1949, 1950, by Sonia Brownell Orwell. Reprinted by permission of Harcourt, Brace Jovanovich, Inc.]

THE CONCLUDING SENTENCE

Be careful not to introduce a new idea or point of view at the end of your paragraph. Under pressure to develop an idea fully, students occasionally add in the final sentence an idea that is only loosely related to the controlling idea and so dissipate the unified impression they have labored to effect. Consider, for example, the following paragraph:

A number of methods for combating juvenile delinquency are currently in use. Some cities punish the parents or guardians of juvenile delinquents by fining or arresting them. The potential delinquent, presumably, would think twice before breaking the law if he knew his mother would be jailed for his crime. In other cities a curfew forbids youths under eighteen to be on the streets after 11 P.M. The National Recreation Association recommends organized leisure-time activities for youths as the best preventative against delinquency. Providing attractive recreational facilities and interesting programs, it is hoped, will keep youngsters off the streets and divert their energies into more constructive channels. A fourth method, the most common, places the juvenile offender in a correctional institution, a reformatory, where an attempt is made to rehabilitate him. All these methods of treating juvenile delinquency have one thing in common—they have all failed. Perhaps the best solution to the problem would be to reestablish a program like the Civilian Conservation Corps that operated in the 1930s.

The writer's purpose in this paragraph, explained in the first sentence, is to discuss various methods for dealing with juvenile delinquency; and in fulfillment of this purpose he describes four methods. In the last sentence, however, she disrupts the unity of this paragraph and weakens her effect by proposing her own solution to juvenile delinquency, the reestablishment of a program similar to the CCC of the depression years. This solution is, clearly, not among the methods currently used to combat juvenile delinquency, and it therefore does not belong in this paragraph. The writer should have reserved it for treatment in another paragraph.

One final suggestion: if you are writing a single paragraph, especially one that is rather long or complex, you can improve its unity by reinforcing the controlling idea in your concluding sentence, as does the writer of the following paragraph:

Essentially, communism is not a simple conspiracy to overthrow the American government, and therefore the FBI is not the primary agency to deal with it. Communism is a theory of social organization that traces historical developments to economic forces. According to Karl Marx, the philosopher and prophet of the Communist movement, history reveals a continuous struggle between social classes for a larger proportion of the wealth produced. In Marx's view the political state is in reality the instrument by which the dominant class, the capitalists, exploits the workers, the proletariat. The laboring class, Marx believes, will have to seize power through violent revolution and establish a temporary dictatorship to create an ideal, classless society. If Marxist doctrine, which has greatly influenced the course of history in the twentieth century, cannot be studied and discussed in American colleges and universities, we shall develop no philosophy to counter communism, no philosophers to do battle with Marxist philosophers, and so yield to them the field. To prevent this we must encourage American college students to study communism and to read books by communists. Communism will be defeated only when its ideas are proven fallacious, and this is a task for teachers, philosophers, statesmen — not policemen.

EXERCISE 4

A. In the following exercise there are three topic sentences, accompanied by a number of supporting sentences. Some of the accompanying sentences directly support the controlling idea of the topic sentence; others are irrelevant. Eliminate the irrelevant sentences and organize those that remain into a paragraph, adding whatever detail may be necessary.

1. Throughout their history Americans have exhibited a thoughtless, savage disregard for the land.

   a. Early settlers discovered a fantastic continent of virgin forests, vast grasslands, and fertile soil.
   b. Treating the land as if it were their enemy, they cut down huge tracts of timber to make room for crops.
   c. This irresponsible attitude toward the land is still evident.
   d. They often abandoned the land when its soil was depleted by wasteful farming practices and moved west to seek new land.
   e. The rich topsoil of the exposed land was carried away by rain water and blown into huge dust clouds by the wind.
   f. Buffalo grass, which covered the plains and protected the soil, was plowed under, exposing the soil to drought and wind.
   g. Strip-mining has ravaged thousands of acres of land in Appalachia.
   h. Heavy rains wash out chemicals from the scarred, denuded land, polluting streams and destroying the fertility of the land that is left.
   i. Conservationists, however, have focused public attention on this disastrous practice, and Congress has passed new laws to control strip-mining.
   j. But the problem is not solved, since Americans will increasingly need coal for energy, and strip-mining is the cheapest way to mine it.
   k. In recent years the construction of freeways has destroyed over one million acres of trees each year.
   l. The loss of these trees aggravates flood conditions during the rainy season because tree roots absorb water and hold soil in place.

2. Conventional standards governing sexual behavior in the United States have been liberalized in recent years.

   a. Evidence of a new sexual permissiveness is evident in the entertainment world.
   b. Former sexual taboos in the motion picture industry have been relaxed to the point that the sex act itself is displayed on the screen.
   c. Sexual references and racy language are much more common in television movies today than they were a few years ago.
   d. Film critics disagree about the artistic value of explicit sex in motion pictures.
   e. Some critics believe explicit sex in films is a sign of health and maturity.
   f. Some critics see the presentation of explicit sex as harmful to the public and damaging to the motion picture as an art form.

g. A few years ago bars and cocktail lounges created a stir by featuring topless waitresses and dancers; today they provide bottomless dancers, as well.

h. It is not unusual to read about motion-picture actresses who have given birth to children out of wedlock and who, moreover, reject the idea of formal marriage ties to legitimize the birth.

i. Traditional attitudes about marriage have been affected; premarital and extramarital sex are more common.

j. The percentage of illegitimate births has risen.

k. A more casual attitude toward sex is evident among the young on college campuses.

l. College infirmaries and clinics now dispense birth control pills to women as a regular service.

m. This liberalizing of sexual mores in the United States may be a healthy sign, a sign that Americans are finally throwing off a repressive attitude toward sex inherited from the Puritans; but it may also be a sign of sickness and decadence.

3. Teachers perform a vital function in our culture today.

a. They perform an essential socializing task by helping children move from the self-contained world of their families to the wider world of school and community.

b. Children must learn to work and play harmoniously in the larger group, adjusting to the environment of a wider social activity, if they are to acquire the foundation for a happy, useful life in a democracy.

c. As the children mature, their teachers help them to develop a receptive attitude toward intellectual pursuits as well as social activities, to respect and respond to the life of the mind.

d. Teachers are largely responsible for transmitting the cultural heritage, the essential knowledge about the political, social, and cultural institutions of the country and of the world.

e. They teach students to discover and develop their own special talents, to acquire vocational skills.

f. When teachers are dedicated to their task, they can strongly influence the moral life of their students.

g. They can help students develop a sound philosophy of life.

h. Yet, in spite of the admitted importance of teachers in our society, their calling is not always valued.

i. They earn considerably less than other professionals — lawyers, doctors, dentists, engineers — and in many states, no more than skilled tradesmen or factory workers.

j. The future of this nation, its place in the community of nations as well as the happiness and well-being of its citizens, is in no small way dependent on how well teachers perform their function.

B. In the following paragraphs the beginning topic sentences have been omitted. Read each paragraph carefully, and then construct a sentence that conveys the main idea of the paragraph.

1. One of the most serious problems affecting these programs is inflation: rising costs of medicine, depreciation of funds available for construction of facilities, increase in doctors' fees. In Sweden, for example, a free, comprehensive dental service enacted by the government had to be revised and the patient forced to pay 50 percent of the bill. Costs for health care have risen sharply in Denmark, Holland, and France as well. Holland even had to suspend medical education temporarily because of lack of money. Another problem is the inevitable bureaucratic ineptness. European critics contend that too much of the doctor's time is spent in filling out forms rather than in administering to the sick, and, as a result, patients must wait longer to see a doctor. Free or inexpensive medicines have resulted in an increase in their use, and the cost of processing prescriptions has risen. Government-backed health programs are not about to collapse in Europe, but they are beset with serious problems that demand attention if the high quality of European medical care is to be maintained.

---

2. First, violence is self-defeating and counterproductive. It creates a mood of repressiveness in Congress, in state legislatures, and in the majority of people, a mood that makes more peaceful, enduring solutions to social problems more difficult to achieve. True, violence may produce some temporary benefits as a result of heightened public awareness of the plight of the poor and the dispossessed, yet in the long run it engenders a backlash, a stiffening of resistance to needed changes in many persons' attitudes toward the rights of minority groups. Second, violence could destroy the whole social fabric of America, and with it, of course, any hope for progress. Any group that justifies violence in support of its own "sincere," "unselfish" aims either ignores or forgets that other groups can do the same. Violence in support of "freedom" will also be used in defense of "order" with tragic consequences.

---

3. Montana State Senator Arnold Rieder early came to the aid of what he called "this gallant little animal." "We wonder," he asked, "if this creature of nature was not meant to have a fairer life. By a twenty-five-to-one ratio the coyote's deeds have been beneficial to man." So did Oklahoma's Senator Gil Graham, who spent a lifetime among Indians and animals. "I consider the coyote," he said, "the most unjustly accused of all animals." Paul Maxwell, another coyote friend, not only aided orphaned and wounded coyote pups in his own house but also quoted his friend Jimmy Siebert, "I ranched sheep for fifty years," Siebert told him, "and I never had a single sheep killed by a coyote." Then too there was Texas rancher Arthur Lytton, who for forty years ran a twenty-thousand-acre spread. "I would never," he said, "allow a preda-

tor to be killed on my land. They are necessary for the balance of nature. Kill them and you're in for nothing but trouble—from rabbits and rodents and everything." [From *Man Kind?* by Cleveland Amory. Harper & Row, Publishers, Inc. 1974, p. 341.]

---

4. What would a society without language be like? It would of course have no writing or other means of communication by words, for all these are ultimately dependent on spoken speech. Our means of learning would therefore be greatly restricted. We should be obliged, like the animals, to learn by doing or by observing the actions of others. All of history would disappear, for without language there would be no way of re-creating past experiences and communicating them to others. We should have no means of expressing our thoughts and ideas to others or of sharing in the mental processes of our fellow-men. Indeed, it is very likely that we should not think at all. Many psychologists maintain that thought itself requires the use of language, that the process of thinking is really talking things over with ourselves. [From Harry Hoijer, "Language in Culture," from *Man, Culture, and Society,* ed. Harry L. Shapiro. Copyright © 1956 by Oxford University Press, Inc. Reprinted by permission.]

C. Examine the following paragraphs for unity and be prepared to point out the specific weakness of those that lack unity and to explain how they might be improved. Check to see that each sentence in the paragraph supports a controlling idea in a topic sentence. As an aid here, enclose the topic sentence of each paragraph in brackets and underline its controlling idea. In those paragraphs that contain primary and secondary support, make certain that each primary statement directly develops the controlling idea and that each secondary statement provides a relevant explanation or clarification of each primary statement. As an aid here, place a capital P before each primary statement and a capital S before each secondary statement. Before every irrelevant sentence place an I.

1. _____Professional boxing should be banned because it is brutal and unsportsmanlike. _____Boxing is the art of attack and defense, with the fists protected by padded gloves. _____It is the art of hitting an opponent without getting hit yourself. _____Good boxing takes control and coordination. _____Pugilism was the first form of boxing. _____It differs from modern boxing because the fist was not padded. _____Boxing in its modern form

began in 1866, when the public became disgusted with the brutality of pugilism.

2. _____The population explosion has brought us up against a number of tough ecological facts. _____Man is at last pressing hard on his spatial environment—there is little leeway left for his colonization of new areas of the world's surface. _____He is pressing hard on his resources, notably non-renewable but also renewable resources. _____As Professor Harrison Brown has so frighteningly made clear in his book, *The Challenge of Man's Future*, ever-increasing consumption by an ever-increasing number of human beings will lead in a very few generations to the exhaustion of all easily exploitable fossil and high-grade mineral ores, to the taking up of all first-rate agricultural land, and so to the invasion of more and more second-rate marginal land for agriculture. _____In fact, we are well on our way to ruining our material habitat. _____But we are beginning to ruin our own spiritual and mental habitat also. _____Not content with destroying or squandering our re-sources of material things, we are beginning to destroy the resources of true enjoyment—spiritual, aesthetic, intellectual, emotional. _____We are spreading great masses of human habitation over the face of the land, neither cities nor suburbs nor towns nor villages, just a vast mass of urban sprawl or subtopia. _____And to escape from this, people are spilling out farther and farther into the wilder parts and so destroying them. _____And we are making our cities so big as to be monstrous, so big that they are becoming impossible to live in. _____Just as there is a maximum possible size for an efficient land animal—you can't have a land animal more than about twice as large as an elephant—so there is a maximum possible efficient size for a city. _____London, New York, and Tokyo have already got beyond that size. [From Julian Huxley, "The Crowded World." Reprinted by permission of A. D. Peters & Co., Ltd.]

3. _____College freshmen face a number of problems as they begin college work. _____If they are not able to solve them, the results can be dis-astrous. _____The most serious problem they face concerns their studies.

_____If they have not learned good study habits in high school, they will be in serious trouble in college, for the range and intensity of college-level subjects make great demands on a student's capacity for concentration. _____All college students should have a place to study that has adequate lighting and that is in a quiet environment. _____They should not try to study while the radio is blaring or the television set is on. _____College freshmen must also learn to budget their time wisely, or they are likely to find that they have concentrated on one or two subjects to the detriment of others. _____Another problem freshmen face concerns extracurricular activities. _____Incoming students sometimes find themselves tempted to attend a dance, a football rally, or a fraternity party when they should be studying. _____Yet, unless they achieve self-discipline, they may find themselves on probation after their first semester. _____Some students, however, seem to need the threat of expulsion to succeed. _____Finally, freshmen must learn to adjust to the rigors of college competition. _____Students who have excelled in their high-school studies become frustrated and depressed when they do not achieve on a similar level in college. _____This keener competition that freshmen face can, if they adapt themselves to it calmly, lead them to a mature understanding of their abilities and limitations. _____Unhappily, it may also lead to serious emotional upset if they set unrealistically high academic goals for themselves.

4. _____The serious depletion of oil and natural gas reserves in the United States has prompted investigation of a number of new sources of energy. _____One of the most promising of these is the fast breeder nuclear reactor. _____The conventional nuclear power plant taps only 1 percent of the energy produced by the splitting (fission) of uranium atoms; and uranium 235, the fuel used, is scarce. _____The fast breeder reactor, however, by a process of transforming uranium into plutonium, produces more fuel than it consumes and therefore virtually eliminates the problem of the scarcity of nuclear fuel. _____An even more fantastic machine now being experimented with is the fusion reactor. _____It combines heavy hydrogen atoms to produce helium

atoms, releasing nuclear energy that can be converted into electricity. _____ Because the fusion reactor uses for fuel an element contained in sea water, the successful development of this device would solve humanity's energy problems for a long, long time. _____Other promising sources of energy are contained in sunlight, subsurface heat, ocean tides, and everyday trash. _____Various experiments are under way to trap sunlight to create heat energy that can be used in boiler turbines to produce electric current. _____ Geothermal power is produced by drilling holes into the earth and forcing cold water into one hole. _____As it comes into contact with hot rock four or five miles below the surface, the water is heated and fractures the rock. _____The hot water then rises to the surface in another hole and is used to drive a turbine to produce electricity. _____In several regions of the world, the ebb and flow of the tides could be harnessed to produce electrical power, as they are on the Rance River estuary in France. _____And, finally, the lowly trash Americans accumulate in ever-increasing quantities, about two and one-half billion tons a year, should not be overlooked. _____Experts estimate that if it were burned in power plants, enough electricity could be generated to take care of 50 percent of this country's current energy needs.

5. _____Critics of America's space exploration program have often described it as an irresponsible, expensive operation that soaks up public funds that could be put to better use, but this view overlooks many substantial achievements of the program. _____Communications satellites have, for example, greatly improved international communication. _____On-the-spot television broadcasting of the 1976 Olympics in Canada dramatically increased interest in the games throughout the world._____Space satellites are also being used to discover mineral resources, to monitor air and water pollution, and to provide better understanding and prediction of the weather. _____The space program has vastly increased man's knowledge. _____The Apollo Program, in particular, has provided much information about the history and formation of the moon, and other programs have provided similar information about other planets. _____Space technology has made possible

the development and manufacture of many useful products. _____ Miniature calculators, improved X-ray machines, better computers, and thousands of other products have been part of the spinoff of the space venture. _____ But perhaps its most significant contribution has been its impetus to the maintenance of America's technological leadership. _____ Fifteen years ago the Soviet Union gained world recognition for its scientific achievement in putting *Sputnik* in orbit, and communism appeared to be the wave of the future.

_____ Since that time, however, consistent American successes in space have reestablished this country's preeminence in this field and prodded the Russians into cooperative space ventures with the Americans. _____ American and Soviet cooperation in space exploration could lead to greater cooperation in other fields and thus enhance chances for world peace. _____ The American investment in space has been expensive, but it has not been irresponsible. _____ In fact, it could prove to have been the wisest investment this country has ever made.

D. In the following short theme the writer describes a high school teacher he liked. Read the two paragraphs carefully at least twice, making certain you understand the dominant impression conveyed by the writer. Then read the material once more, this time noting specific details of appearance and action that communicate this impression.

Mr. Turner

I liked most of my high school teachers. They were for the most part friendly and competent, willing to help any student who showed the faintest flicker of interest in their subjects. I liked them—but I do not remember them very distinctly, except for Mr. Turner, my physiology teacher. He was a lively, eccentric little man, five feet five inches in his bare feet, with a freckled, bald head. When he smiled, his mouth stretched from ear to ear, and his eyes sparkled brightly. If a student went to Mr. Turner after class and asked a question that pleased him, he would grasp the student firmly by the elbow, knit his brows in furious concentration as he formulated an answer, and relax into a grin as his questioner nodded his head in understanding. He spoke with a slight lisp, which became pronounced whenever he was upset, as he was whenever he had to speak somewhat harshly to discipline a student. Once during an examination, Ben Sanders, who played right tackle on our football team, crept stealthily across the classroom floor to give a fellow athlete a "hot foot." Mr. Turner spotted him and, with a glint of determination in his eyes, tiptoed behind him and tapped him on the shoulder. As Ben rather sheepishly straightened up, Mr. Turner eyed him intensely. "Mr. Thanders," he said, spraying Ben with a saliva mist, "pleath thee me after clath." We all laughed, not disrespectfully, but because of the incongruity of our diminutive teacher disciplining a student who towered fourteen inches over him (and weighed 100 pounds more).

That year Mr. Turner turned sixty-five, and he retired from teaching in June. The day before the final examination, his last day of teaching after forty-three years, he spoke to us briefly, his lisp slightly more noticeable than usual because of the emotion of the moment. He praised our attentiveness—he nodded slightly in the direction of Ben Sanders—and our progress. He said he had finally decided what he wanted to do in life, and he looked forward to retirement so he could get on with it. As I recall, he said he had always wanted to work in a dental laboratory, and he had gotten a job helping to make false teeth in a dentist friend's laboratory. As he finished speaking, we all clapped and stood up. As we walked out, he grasped each of us by the hand and elbow and wished us well. I can still see him, beaming and nodding his head as I wished him good luck.

The central impression here is that of a "lively, eccentric little man." This controlling idea is explicitly expressed in the fourth sentence. The preceding three sentences provide background information. Succeeding sentences contain the pictorial details that convey the picture of a likable and energetic, though eccentric, teacher—his size, smile, firm grasp, and lisp. Two incidents are included, one involving Ben Sanders and the other concerning Mr. Turner's retirement plans, that provide further concrete illustration of the controlling idea. Think back over your own experiences, and select a person who has made a strong impression on you—a relative, a friend, a teacher, an employer. Write a brief paper of one or two paragraphs in which you present a unified impression of that individual. Select your details carefully, using only those that directly relate to the impression you wish to convey.

E. Read the following poem carefully, at least twice. It is carefully constructed to present a dominant impression of a man, Richard Cory. Though he is shown to have several admirable qualities, they are all related to one overriding quality. What is that quality? What adjective best describes him? Bear in mind that you are not asked to relate the message of the poem, its central idea, but only the dominant quality of Richard Cory. Is the name Richard Cory well chosen? Why? How does it reinforce his dominant quality?

Richard Cory[*]

Whenever Richard Cory went down town,
We people on the pavement looked at him:
He was a gentleman from sole to crown,
Clean favored, and imperially slim.

[*] By Edwin Arlington Robinson

And he was always quietly arrayed,
And he was always human when he talked;
But still he fluttered pulses when he said,
"Good-morning," and he glittered when he walked.

And he was rich—yes, richer than a king—
And admirably schooled in every grace:
In fine, we thought that he was everything
To make us wish that we were in his place.

So on we worked, and waited for the light,
And went without the meat, and cursed the bread;
And Richard Cory, one calm summer night,
Went home and put a bullet through his head.

SUMMARY

The most important quality of good writing is clarity. To achieve clarity and conciseness in your paragraphs, you must make sure they are unified. The following suggestions will help you write unified paragraphs:

1. Be sure that each paragraph has a controlling idea expressed in a topic sentence. As a check against irrelevancy, it is helpful to place this sentence at the beginning of a paragraph, but occasionally it may be placed elsewhere—at the end of a paragraph, for example, to summarize rather than to announce a topic.

2. Make certain that primary supporting detail focuses clearly on the controlling idea.

3. If the central idea requires more than primary support, make certain that secondary supporting detail explains and clarifies the primary detail.

4. Be especially careful to avoid inserting a new idea in the last sentence of the paragraph.

CHAPTER TWO | Development

A second important quality of an effective paragraph is complete-ness. A major weakness in student writing is the underdevelopment of paragraphs, the failure to supply sufficient detail to clarify, illus-trate, or support the controlling idea. Because the paragraph is an organic entity—a group of related sentences that develop a single idea—it must be reasonably complete if it is to communicate this idea satisfactorily. Consider, for example, the following paragraph:

> The notion that the only valuable knowledge to be acquired in college is that which can be put to some practical use is mistaken. Students who limit their choice of subjects to those emphasizing the acquisition of technical skill restrict their opportunities for in-tellectual growth and stimulation. College students should there-fore not avoid the liberal arts in their choice of subjects.

This paragraph begins with a clear, concise topic sentence, but the paragraph is incomplete, for the topic sentence has not been fully developed. The only argument offered to support the idea that a con-centration on practical subjects is mistaken is that such a focus in-hibits intellectual growth and stimulation. Moreover, the argument is not substantiated. The writer should have explained how or why intellectual growth is inhibited, and should have offered other argu-ments as well. The writer of this paragraph has simply not said enough about the controlling idea. By adding clarifying detail and supporting arguments, he or she could have developed the controlling idea more fully and made the thesis more persuasive. Here is a revised version:

> The notion that the only valuable knowledge to be acquired in college is that which can be put to some practical use is mistaken.

37

Students who limit their choice of subjects to those emphasizing the acquisition of technical skill restrict their opportunities for intellectual growth and stimulation. Courses that train students to build a computer, manage a business, or design a turbine engine are of course useful. Modern civilization would not be possible without them. But an exclusive concentration on utilitarian subjects narrows a student's range of interests and produces inward-looking individuals. Liberal studies — philosophy, art, literature, history, law — however, lead outward to the great network of ideas that have stimulated men's minds for centuries. They expose students to fundamental questions about the nature of humanity and society, about the ends of human life. They help students to learn to see themselves in their proper perspective apart from purely personal concerns. The liberal studies thus provide a balance to the technical studies. They also open avenues and outlets that students can pursue in later life apart from their work. The increasing productivity of machines promises a future of abundant leisure, but added leisure time will be tedious for those without a range of intelligent interests and activities.

This second version is more convincing because its controlling idea has been more fully developed. The original argument that a concentration on technical subjects inhibits intellectual growth has been clarified by contrasting the direction of liberal studies with that of technical studies. And a second argument has been added: nontechnical subjects stimulate interests that students can pursue later on in life in their leisure time.

The more fully developed the paragraph, the longer it will be, as in the example above; but there is no set length for a paragraph. In expository writing the majority of paragraphs consist of clusters of sentences that develop one idea. The writer, having finished with one aspect of the subject, moves on to another aspect in a new paragraph. Occasionally, however, factors other than thought movement influence paragraph length. Newspaper paragraphs, for example, often consist of only one sentence. The narrow-column format makes it necessary to reduce paragraph length to make it easier for the reader to digest information. Considerations of rhythm and emphasis may also dictate shorter paragraphs, particularly in the longer essay or article. A short paragraph sandwiched between longer ones may provide a change of pace, a chance for readers to pause slightly and assimilate what they have read before continuing; or it may underscore an important point, the contrast in paragraph size focusing the readers' attention. And introductory or concluding paragraphs may also be short for similar reasons. The kinds of expository paragraphs you will be required to write, however, usually demand 100 to 150 words (six to ten sentences) for adequate development. But regardless of paragraph length, your main concern will be to include sufficient detail so that your readers can comprehend your meaning without having to supply their own information.

The ability to write well-developed paragraphs requires a good deal of practice in thought development. The quality of your paragraphs will depend largely on your ability to think of effective ways to illustrate and support your ideas. A ready supply of ideas is therefore a basic asset to any writer. However, this supply is seldom available to the average college freshman. You are certainly not abnormal, therefore, if you have had trouble finding material to support your ideas in a written assignment. But you can do something about it. You can increase your stock of ideas and your fund of information and thereby facilitate your thinking and your writing.

One way of doing this is through reading—newspapers, weekly news magazines, books. Your studies will provide ample opportunity for improving your reading skills, but you will find that the news and editorial sections of first-rate newspapers and news magazines are especially valuable sources of ideas and information. When you need information on a specific subject, consult the *Readers' Guide to Periodical Literature,* a library reference work that alphabetically lists magazine articles by subject and by authors' last names. Listening to radio and television news commentators and conversing with persons knowledgeable in particular subjects will also provide information and insight.

What you learn through reading, listening, and conversing will increase your stock of ideas. But what you learn in these ways needs to be related to what you know firsthand—what you have learned from your own experience, your own feelings, impressions, and reflections—if it is to become a permanent part of your intellect. To record their impressions and reactions to what they have read and observed, professional writers frequently keep a journal. By writing down their thoughts and impressions, they can retain what might otherwise be forgotten. As a beginning writer you will also find it useful to keep a journal and to record your responses to events; for it can serve as the seedbed in which ideas for future paragraphs and essays will germinate.

Your journal need not be a formal one. A simple notebook in which you jot down phrases, sentences, or more extended ideas will suffice. Your entries might look something like these:

1/15/77   Lincoln wrote that progress is brought about by unreasonable men. This is probably true. Those who fought for free public schooling a hundred years ago were probably considered "weird." On the other hand, not all unreasonable men improve things. Hitler, Mussolini, Stalin were unreasonable.

1/22/77   "The future," as one politician once put it, "lies ahead." It may not, after all; for ecologists tell us that the highly industrialized American economy has created serious problems for our survival by using so many of the world's exhaustible resources and polluting the atmosphere. Yet economists argue that the only way underdeveloped nations can improve the lot of their people is through greater industrialization of their economies, which means that these countries will steadily devour more natural resources and pollute the environment, too.

1/25/77   It is ironic that those who would destroy the American "Establishment" with fire or bombs frequently speak of the need for love and unity in the world. Santayana wrote, "Fanaticism consists in redoubling your effort when you have forgotten your aim."

Keeping a journal will obviously not transform you in one semester into a thoughtful, prolific writer. It will not immediately solve the problem of gathering ideas for interesting paragraphs, but it will, if seriously undertaken, force you to think more clearly and to become more sensitive and responsive to your experience. It will force you to express those vague, half-formed notions in writing and thus clarify and fix them in your mind. In the discussion that follows you will see examples of well-written paragraphs. By studying and imitating these common patterns of paragraph development, you will learn some simple techniques for expanding an idea into a fully formed paragraph.

Your choice of method in developing a paragraph will usually be determined by your topic sentence. That is, a well-written topic sentence generally implies a method of development. Consider the following topic sentence:

The farmer's income increased dramatically between 1940 and 1946.

This statement obviously calls for factual detail to support it. Now consider the following sentence:

Slang is frequently vivid and expressive.

Here one certainly needs illustrative detail. Consider this sentence:

> The political labels "conservative" and "reactionary" are frequently confused in political discussions today.

This statement clearly requires a combination of definition, comparison, and contrast to develop it adequately.

In the following pages several patterns or ways of developing expository paragraphs are discussed and illustrated: (1) illustration, (2) factual detail, (3) comparison and contrast, (4) analysis, (5) definition, and (6) combination of methods. The first two — illustration and factual detail — are, together with reasons or judgments, the basic materials of which most expository paragraphs are constructed. The others represent common methods of organizing facts, judgments, and illustrations to construct a paragraph. (Developing a paragraph by the use of reasons will be considered later in a discussion of the argumentative paragraph.) This list does not include all the possible methods of developing paragraphs, but it does offer a variety of frequently used patterns that should give you some guidance.

1. ILLUSTRATION

An easy and effective way to support an idea is to use examples. The writer makes a statement and then clarifies it through illustrative detail: he points to a specific occurrence, condition, or fact that concretely illustrates his idea. In your paragraphs you may decide to use only one carefully sustained example to support your controlling idea, as the writer of the following paragraph does:

> Comedies that were once madcap have turned sour. Take *The Out-of-Towners* (1970), which, as written by Neil Simon, detailed the luckless adventures of a couple from Ohio who pay New York a visit so that the husband can be interviewed for an executive job that would require moving to the metropolis. First off, their plane is stacked up over LaGuardia, then diverted to Boston. The train they are forced to take to New York carries no food. In the city there are taxi and transit strikes, so they must walk to their hotel through garbage-littered streets (there is also a sanitation strike) in drenching rain. Because of lateness they lose their hotel reservation. On the way to find other quarters they are mugged and robbed. In Central Park they are assaulted by weirdos and, reduced to near starvation, they battle with a dog for the remains of a child's box of Cracker Jacks. In spite of all this, the husband manages to keep

his job appointment, but understandably he's had enough. He turns down the offer and thankfully heads back to Ohio. [From Hollis Alpert, "Indecent Exposures," *Saturday Review*, November 7, 1972. Reprinted by permission.]

Or you may use several examples as the writer of the following paragraph does to illustrate the hardihood of the raccoon:

Nothing about him is rare, delicate, or specialized. He is as common as dirt and as hardy as weeds. When wild chestnuts disappear he switches to acorns and hazelnuts; when his den trees are cut down he moves into fox burrows, culverts, caves, and old barns; in the deep South he is active all year, but he sleeps through Northern winters; where the sea provides shellfish he abandons his nocturnal habits and fishes in broad daylight following the ebb tide. He lives in suburbs, sleeping in attics and raiding garbage cans. He develops a rich, heavy coat for Canadian winters, and a thin, almost white one for the hot brilliance of the Florida Keys. He eats crayfish in Ohio swamplands, and on Cape Sable he must dig wells down to fresh water. In Michigan he is an important cash crop and in Florida he is a pest. [From Polly Redford, "Our Most American Animal," *Harper's Magazine*, 1963. Reprinted by permission of McIntosh and Otis, Inc.]

In general, several examples are more convincing than one. But a carefully chosen example, one that clearly illustrates and is honestly representative, is preferable to a series of superficial, atypical ones. If your controlling idea is fairly complex, it is probably better to use one extended example so that you have ample opportunity to develop your idea fully. In either case, the important point is that your examples be clear, relevant, and as specific as possible.

A pattern of development similar to illustration is the use of an anecdote—a short narrative of some incident, frequently personal or biographical—to illustrate an idea. In the following paragraph William H. Whyte, Jr., uses an anecdote to illustrate his belief that executives of modern companies value the genial, cooperative employee more than the man of genius.

Even when companies recognize that they are making a choice between brilliance and mediocrity, it is remarkable how excruciating they find the choice. Several years ago my colleagues and I listened to the management of an electronics company hold a postmortem on a difficult decision they had just made. The company had been infiltrated by genius. Into their laboratory three years before had come a very young, brilliant man. He did magnificent work and the company looked for even greater things in the future. But, though he was a likable fellow, he was imaginative and he had begun to chafe at the supervision of the research director. The director, the management said, was a rather run-of-the-mill sort, though he had worked loyally and congenially for the company. Who would have to be sacrificed? Reluctantly, the company made its decision. The brilliant man would have to go. The management was unhappy about the decision but they argued that harmonious group thinking (this was the actual word they used) was the company's prime aim, and if they had promoted the brilliant man it would have upset the whole chain of company interpersonal relationships. What else, they asked plaintively, could they have done? [From William H. Whyte, Jr., "The Fight Against Genius," *The Organization Man,* Simon and Schuster, Inc., pp. 213–14. Copyright © 1956 by William H. Whyte, Jr.]

When you use an anecdote to illustrate your controlling idea, make certain that it is concise and to the point. Do not develop it to such length that the reader forgets the point it was intended to support.

The following paragraphs all use some form of illustration to develop a thought. In the first paragraph the writer illustrates the war-like aspects of professional football.

The players know what it is. "Pro football is the closest thing you can get to all-out war," Baltimore's quarterback, Johnny Unitas, says. "It is physical combat. In place of weapons, they use hands, forearms, shoulders, and anything else they've got to get at you. Thank God they don't have guns out there, but sometimes I wish I had one." The coaches call it "contact." We may define it with a better word, *violence.* Pittsburgh's fullback, John Henry Johnson, for example, once hit the Cardinals' Charley Trippi with a blind side block that fractured Trippi's skull and broke his nose. He tackled a teammate during a practice scrimmage, breaking the man's jaw in two places. And another time, after he had broken the jaw of Les Richter of the Rams, Johnson himself was knocked flat and set upon by four of Richter's teammates. Johnson jumped to his feet, yanked a steel sideline marker out of the ground, and began clubbing his attackers before the referees stopped the fight. Green Bay's middle linebacker, Ray Nitschke, once tackled a halfback so hard that the man lay unconscious for ten minutes after he was carried off the field into the locker room. The Bear's right end, Mike Ditka, has a straight arm like a jousting pole; a defensive back once grabbed the arm and was dragged twenty-five yards across his own goal line.

And the Detroit Lions' defensive tackle Roger Brown, who weighs three hundred pounds, once stopped quarterback Billy Wade of the Chicago Bears by actually throwing a Bear blocker at him. The unfortunate flying Bear weighed two hundred forty-three pounds. [From Thomas B. Morgan, "The American War Game," *Esquire Magazine,* October, 1965, pp. 78–79.]

In the next paragraph the writer uses several examples.

But Pidgin's seemingly imprecise vocabulary can be almost poetic at times. There could hardly be, in any language, a friendlier definition of a friend than the Australian aborigine's "him brother belong me." Or consider his description of the sun: "lamp belong Jesus." Pidgin can be forthright, too. An Aussie policeman is "gub-mint catchum-fella." An elbow is "screw belong arm." Whiskers are "grass belong face." When a man gets old there, he is "no more too much strong." When he's thirsty, "him belly allatime burn." Even the English language is a little spicier today for the inclusion of a good many expressions borrowed from Pidgin, though few who use them are aware of their origin. Among them: chow, make-do, savvy, can do (and no can do), pickaninny, joss, and look-see. [Copyright © 1963 by Gary Jennings. First published in *Harper's Magazine* in an article entitled "Pidgin: No Laughing Matter."]

Gloria Steinem, a leader in the Women's Liberation movement in the United States, uses illustration to support her contention that in an ideal society men and women would choose rather than simply accept their roles.

Men will have to give up ruling-class privileges, but in return they will no longer be the only ones to support the family, get drafted, bear the strain of power and responsibility. Freud to the contrary, anatomy is not destiny, at least not for more than nine months at a time. In Israel, women are drafted, and some have gone to war. In England, more men type and run switchboards. In India and Israel, a woman rules. In Sweden, both parents take care of the children. In this country, come Utopia, men and women won't reverse roles: they will be free to choose according to individual talents and preferences. [From Gloria Steinem, "What It Would Be Like If Women Win," *Time,* August 31, 1970, p. 22. Reprinted by permission from *Time, The Weekly Newsmagazine.* Copyright Time, Inc., 1970.]

EXERCISE 5

A. Write a paragraph of 100 to 150 words on one of the topics listed below, and use examples to develop it. As you plan your paragraph, transform the topic into a sharply defined, specific idea and express it as your topic sentence. Then list all the examples you can remember from your own experience or reading—consult your journal here—that might be used to develop your controlling idea. As you consider your supporting detail, you may wish to modify your original topic sentence. Do not hesitate to do so. Formulating a topic sentence at the beginning is simply a way of ensuring unity. After you have eliminated irrelevancies from your list, write your paragraph and make certain that the illustrations you present in support of your controlling idea are clear, concrete, and interesting. (Use this procedure in planning your paragraphs for the exercises that follow each section of this chapter.)

1. violence in professional sports, motion pictures, or television programs
2. embarrassing moments (use an anecdote)
3. a friend with an unusual trait
4. misleading commercials
5. strengths or weaknesses in American life
6. ways of conserving energy in the United States
7. advantages or disadvantages of urban living
8. chauvinism in the United States
9. American life as reflected in motion pictures, television programs
10. American lifestyles

B. The following quoted passages contain interesting subjects for paragraphs. Select one, explain its meaning, and provide illustrations to support your interpretation. Use your first sentence to introduce the quotation.

1. It is a true proverb, that if you live with a lame man, you will learn to limp.   —Plutarch
2. Fortune is like the market, when many times, if you can stay a little, the price will fall.   —Francis Bacon
3. It is foolish to fear the thorns when one beholds the rose.   —Arabic proverb
4. He who would speak the truth must have one foot in the stirrup.   —Turkish proverb
5. It seems to me that the only law which there is any merit in obeying is the one you do not agree with. . . .   —Lord Hailsham, Britain's Lord High Chancellor
6. Man's capacity for justice makes democracy possible; but man's inclination to injustice makes democracy necessary.   —Reinhold Niebuhr
7. The optimist proclaims that we live in the best of all possible worlds, and the pessimist fears this is true.   —James Branch Cabell

2. FACTUAL DETAIL

Factual detail is often used to support an idea. The writer may begin a paragraph with a topic statement and then support that statement with facts and statistics. Or the writer may present the details first and place the topic sentence at the end as the logical conclusion to be drawn from the evidence. The following paragraph is arranged with the topic idea at the beginning.

Of some 200 million tons of waste poured into the air each year, automotive vehicles contribute 94.6 million tons. What flows out of an automobile exhaust pipe is a mixture of five principal gases and chemicals, none of them good: carbon monoxide, sulphur oxide, hydrocarbons, various oxides of nitrogen and tiny particles of lead. When the exhaust products of 4 million cars are trapped in a basin such as Los Angeles and acted upon by strong sunlight, the result is photochemical oxidant, better known as smog. Arie Hagen-Smit, a Caltech biochemist, identified in 1950 the most harmful ingredients in the whisky-brown air as ozone, PAN (peroxyacl nitrate) and nitrogen dioxide. Ozone, a form of oxygen, is very reactive chemically, bleaching anything it touches, causing dead spots on leaves, cracking rubber and deteriorating cotton fabrics. PAN causes the eye irritation without which no smog would be complete, as well as the acrid odor; nitrogen dioxide provides the color—and damage to lung tissue. [From "The Ravaged Environment," *Newsweek*, January 26, 1970, p. 37. Copyright Newsweek, Inc., January, 1970. All rights reserved. Reprinted by permission.]

Because both facts and judgments are useful in supporting topic sentences, and because confusion between the two sometimes weakens student writing, a brief explanation of their differences should be instructive. A fact is a report, a statement of what has actually happened or of what actually exists. It can be verified: one can test the accuracy of the report through one's own observation or computation or by consulting a reliable source. For example, the following statement is factual:

Jimmy Carter defeated Gerald Ford in the 1976 presidential election.

A judgment, on the other hand, records a personal opinion. It indicates approval or disapproval. Unlike a factual statement, it cannot be
proven true or false. The following statement is judgmental:

Lyndon Johnson was an effective president.

Many statements, however, cannot be so precisely differentiated as
these two examples. The following statement involves both fact and
judgment:

Mountain climbing is an arduous activity.

It can be verified to an extent, and yet it clearly includes judgment.
In your writing make certain that your paragraphs do not consist
solely of judgments unsupported by facts. Judgments can serve both
as topic sentences and as supporting detail, but they need to be
grounded in, and illustrated by, facts if they are to be convincing.
The student who wrote the following paragraph, for example, relied
too heavily on judgment unsupported by fact to prove his point.

Plea bargaining, a negotiated agreement between the lawyer of
the accused and the prosecuting attorney whereby the accused
agrees to plead guilty to a lesser crime than the one he or she is
charged with so as to avoid a possibly stiffer sentence, is corrupting
the administration of criminal justice in the United States. Supporters of this practice claim that it is an efficient technique, saves
the cost of a trial, and gives the defendant a break. In fact, however,
it is simply a perversion of justice that puts criminals back on the
streets to prey on society. The criminal justice system in the United
States is in a mess because of plea bargaining. Those who defend
the practice must bear a good share of the blame.

Such words and phrases as "corrupting," "perversion of justice,"
"prey on society," and "must bear a good share of the blame" express
the writer's judgment. This judgment is not supported with facts,
however. A revised version, with factual statements added, is more
persuasive.

I do not believe that plea bargaining represents a step forward
for criminal justice in this country. This practice, whereby the
accused agrees to plead guilty to a lesser crime than the one he or
she is charged with so as to avoid a possibly stiffer sentence, has
become an integral part of the administration of American criminal
procedure. In 1974, for example, almost 68 percent of the criminal

cases handled by the Los Angeles Superior Court, 13,294 out of 19,608, were processed by means of plea bargaining.* Those who defend the practice—a group that includes numerous courts, the American Bar Association, and legal commissions—argue that plea bargaining is an efficient technique, saves court costs, and gives the defendant a break. It is true that eliminating plea bargaining would increase the cost of criminal justice: it has been estimated that the number of judges, prosecutors, public defenders—all those needed to try a defendant in a public trial—would have to be more than doubled.† The cost of such an increase, it must be admitted, would be substantial; but the present system, which puts criminals back on the street sooner, is, in the long run, far most costly to society. And this cost includes more than the loss or destruction of property. It includes the loss of innocent lives as well. The argument that plea bargaining gives the defendant a break is undeniable. But the "break" he or she gets in the form of more lenient treatment from prosecutors and judges is not a break for society, whose interests also deserve to be protected. And, finally, plea bargaining distorts justice because it is removed from public view in an open court where the interests of society and the rights of the defendant can be more effectively protected. "Too often," writes Gene Blake, a legal affairs writer for the *Los Angeles Times,* "some private defense lawyers who depend on a volume of small criminal cases for their livelihood and public defenders with too many cases to handle may urge guilty pleas which are not in the best interest of possibly innocent clients."‡ The best that can be said of plea bargaining is that it compensates for the failures of an inefficient criminal justice system. If this system is to function effectively in the future, however, other means must be found to sustain it.

The central proposition is more soundly argued in this revision, for several facts have been supplied to bolster the judgments of the original. Although the reader may still reject the proposition, he is aware of the evidence that led the writer to his conclusion.

The following paragraphs provide further illustration of the use of factual detail as supporting material.

Such a drastic shift in U.S. policy in the Middle East is hardly on the horizon today. Still, the potential clout of the Arab oil nations is nothing short of awesome. "If nothing changes," observes

---

* Gene Blake, "Trial System Debate Is On in California," *Los Angeles Times,* 9 November 1975, Part VIII, p. 5.
† Ibid.
‡ Ibid.

Walter Levy, a New York-based oil consultant, "by 1980 the U.S. will be dependent on the Mideast for up to 55 percent of its oil imports, and Western Europe and Japan will be dependent on the same area for some 75 to 80 percent of theirs." Such a lock on the market would make the treasuries of many Arab states almost as supersaturated with hard currency reserves as their deserts are with oil. Saudi Arabia alone would have $30 billion in gold and hard currency by 1983 (by contrast, the U.S. today has only $13 billion in monetary reserves), and Libya, with only 2 million people, is now sitting on $3 billion in reserves. Notes Levy: "They are converting a liquid Fort Knox underground to a solid Fort Knox aboveground." [From "Liquid Gold = Fluid Politics," *Newsweek*, February 19, 1973, p. 49. Copyright Newsweek, Inc. 1973. All rights reserved. Reprinted by permission.]

The statistics on child criminals are awesome. Juvenile crime has risen by 1,600 per cent in twenty years. More crimes are committed by children under 15 than by adults over 25 — indeed, some authorities calculate that half of all crimes in the nation are committed by juveniles. Last year, police arrested 2.5 million youngsters under 18. In Los Angeles, juveniles account for more than one-third of all major crimes, and in Phoenix, officials estimate that juveniles are responsible for 80 per cent of law violations. In Atlanta, juvenile arrests for arson have tripled since 1970, and in New York, since 1972, burglary and rape charges against juveniles have nearly doubled. [From "Children and the Law," *Newsweek*, September 8, 1975, p. 66. Copyright 1975 by Newsweek, Inc. All rights reserved. Reprinted by permission.]

EXERCISE 6

A. The controlling idea in each of the following sentences could be developed into a paragraph with supporting factual detail. Consult reference works in the library and supply several facts in support of each idea. List your data in the spaces provided.

1. Income tax laws permit individuals in the higher brackets to reduce their taxes through a variety of tax shelter schemes.

_____

_____

_____

_____

2. The productive capacity of American farmers is awesome.

_____

_____

_____

_____

3. Annual per capita income in the United States is among the highest in the world.

_____

_____

_____

_____

4. The performance of Olympic track and field athletes has improved enormously over the past fifty years.

_____

_____

_____

_____

B. Select one of the four topic sentences given in A and, using the factual information you have listed, write a paragraph of 100 words or more.

51

3. COMPARISON AND CONTRAST

In paragraphs of *comparison* writers point out similarities between two or more things. In paragraphs of *contrast* they point out the differences. As a student you will frequently be asked to compare or contrast philosophical ideas, historical figures, characters in a novel, or political parties. By studying these two patterns carefully and by practicing the techniques involved, you can improve your ability to develop and communicate your thought clearly.

The supporting material for comparison or contrast frequently consists of factual details, judgments, or examples. In the following paragraph the writer points up the resemblance in the character of the American Southerner and the Afrikaner (an inhabitant of South Africa born of white — usually Dutch — parents) and supports the comparison by a series of factual statements:

Quite apart from the color problem, there are strong resemblances in the character of the American Southerner and the Afrikaner in South Africa; they were molded by the same kind of history and sociology. Both societies have developed from the isolation of the frontier, with the gun, the Bible, and the ox-cart as their powerful symbols. Both have a stern Calvinist tradition, a lingering belief that they are a "chosen race," and a sense of guilt augmented by the habit of miscegenation. In both continents, the richer whites have a slow patriarchal charm, fostered by heat and leisure; while the poor whites have a violent roughness, alternating between hatred for the Negro and real sympathy and understanding for him. [From Anthony Sampson, "Little Rock & Johannesburg," *Nation*, January 10, 1959, pp. 23–24.]

The next paragraph presents an English writer's view of two kinds of confidence displayed by women. The controlling idea, expressed in the first sentence, is supported by judgments and an analogy.

With the two kinds of femininity go two kinds of confidence: there are the women who are cocksure, and the women who are hensure. A really up-to-date woman is a cocksure woman. She doesn't have a doubt nor a qualm. She is a modern type. Whereas the old-fashioned demure woman was sure as a hen is sure, that is, without knowing anything about it. She went quietly and busily clucking around, laying the eggs and mothering the chickens in a kind of anxious dream that still was full of sureness. But not mental sureness. Her sureness was a physical condition, very soothing, but a condition out of which she could easily be startled or frightened. [From D. H. Lawrence, "Cocksure Women and Hensure Men," in *Phoenix II: Uncollected, Unpublished and Other Prose Works by D. H. Lawrence*, edited by Warren Roberts and Harry T. Moore. Copyright 1928 by Forum Publishing Co., copyright © renewed 1956 by Frieda Lawrence Ravagli. All rights reserved. Reprinted by permission of The Viking Press, Inc.]

The distinction between a child's play and an adult's phantasies is the subject of the next paragraph. Supporting material represents the judgments of the writer, Sigmund Freud.

People's phantasies are less easy to observe than the play of children. The child, it is true, plays by himself or forms a closed psychical system with other children for the purposes of a game; but even though he may not play his game in front of the grown-ups, he does not, on the other hand, conceal it from them. The adult, on the contrary, is ashamed of his phantasies and hides them from other people. He cherishes his phantasies as his most intimate possessions, and as a rule he would rather confess his misdeeds than tell anyone his phantasies. It may come about that for that reason he believes he is the only person who invents such phantasies and has no idea that creations of this kind are widespread among other people. This difference in the behaviour of a person who plays and a person who phantasies is accounted for by the motives of these two activities, which are nevertheless adjuncts to each other. [From Sigmund Freud, "Creative Writers and Day-Dreaming," Chapter IX, *Collected Papers of Sigmund Freud,* Volume 4, Authorized translation under the supervision of Joan Riviere, published by Basic Books, Inc., by arrangement with The Hogarth Press Ltd. and The Institute of Psycho-Analysis, London.]

The pattern of development of the following paragraph includes both comparison and contrast. The writer discusses the similarities and contrasts in character and political views of Nikolai Lenin, first premier of the U.S.S.R., and William Gladstone, British statesman and prime minister in the late nineteenth century.

Lenin, with whom I had a long conversation in Moscow in 1920, was, superficially, very unlike Gladstone, and yet, allowing for the difference of time and place and creed, the two men had much in common. To begin with the differences: Lenin was cruel, which

Gladstone was not; Lenin had no respect for tradition, whereas Gladstone had a great deal; Lenin considered all means legitimate for securing the victory of his party, whereas for Gladstone politics was a game with certain rules that must be observed. All these differences, to my mind, are to the advantage of Gladstone, and accordingly Gladstone on the whole had beneficient effects, while Lenin's effects were disastrous. In spite of all these dissimilarities, however, the points of resemblance were quite as profound. Lenin supposed himself to be an atheist, but in this he was mistaken. He thought that the world was governed by the dialectic, whose instrument he was; just as much as Gladstone, he conceived of himself as the human agent of a superhuman Power. His ruthlessness and unscrupulousness were only as to means, not as to ends; he would not have been willing to purchase personal power at the expense of apostasy. Both men derived their personal force from this unshakable conviction of their own rectitude. Both men, in support of their respective faiths, ventured into realms in which, from ignorance, they could only cover themselves with ridicule — Gladstone in Biblical criticism, Lenin in philosophy. [From "Eminent Men I Have Known," in *Unpopular Essays*. Copyright © 1950, by Bertrand Russell. Reprinted by permission of Simon & Schuster, Inc.]

Arrangement of Supporting Material

You may arrange the supporting material for a paragraph based on comparison or contrast in a variety of ways. If you are comparing two persons, for example, you may present the information about the first person in the first four or five sentences and the information about the second person in the remaining sentences. The paragraph below illustrates this method. Feminine and masculine body behavior are contrasted; each is described in a block of sentences:

Such patterns of masculine and feminine body behavior vary widely from one culture to another. In America, for example, women stand with their thighs together. Many walk with their pelvis tipped slightly forward and their upper arms close to their body. When they sit, they cross their legs at the knee or, if they are well past middle age, they may cross their ankles. American men hold their arms away from their body, often swinging them as they walk. They stand with their legs apart (an extreme example is the cowboy, with legs apart and thumbs tucked into the belt). When they sit, they put their feet on the floor with legs apart and, in some parts of the country, they cross their legs by putting one ankle on the other knee. [From Edward and Mildred Hall, "The Sounds of Silence," *Playboy,* June, 1971.]

Another method is to alternate between subjects in successive sentences, as does this writer who compares Hamlet with Abraham Lincoln:

Hamlet feigned insanity for a purpose, and the commentators have written volumes trying to decide whether the deception did not in the end become grim reality. Lincoln struggled out of his despairing mood, put the ghost of little Ann Rutledge in the back of his mind with the equally lovely ghost of universal righteousness, married Mary Todd, compromised with many expediences, composed the Gettysburg Address and the Second Inaugural, and saved the Union. Hamlet went down in the muck of circumstances. . . . [From "Great Individuals," an editorial in *The New York Times*, October 22, 1938, copyright 1938 by The New York Times Company. Reprinted by permission.]

A third method is to deal with the objects in the same sentence, as Anthony Sampson does in comparing the American Southerner with the Afrikaner:

Both societies have developed from the isolation of the frontier, with the gun, the Bible, and the ox-cart as their powerful symbols. Both have a stern Calvinist tradition. . . .

And, of course, it is possible to combine these various methods, as Bertrand Russell does in the paragraph in which he compares and contrasts Lenin with Gladstone. In the second and third sentences of that paragraph, the author deals with both subjects in the same sentence:

To begin with the differences: Lenin was cruel, which Gladstone was not; Lenin had no respect for tradition, whereas Gladstone had a great deal. . . . All these differences, to my mind, are to the advantage of Gladstone, and accordingly Gladstone on the whole had beneficent effects, while Lenin's effects were disastrous. . . .

However, in the fifth, sixth, and seventh sentences he focuses primarily on Lenin:

Lenin supposed himself to be an atheist, but in this he was mistaken. He thought . . . Power. His ruthlessness . . . apostasy.

And in the final sentences he deals with both men in the same sentence.

In a composition of several paragraphs you will have a similar choice in arranging detail. For example, if you were contrasting Los Angeles with Milwaukee on the basis of educational opportunities, recreational facilities, and variety of industries, you might focus on Los Angeles in the first few paragraphs, each paragraph dealing with one of these three points, and then consider Milwaukee in the remaining paragraphs; or you might discuss educational opportunities, recreational facilities, and variety of industries in this order, shifting your focus between Los Angeles and Milwaukee as you progressed. In compositions of several pages, it is probably more effective to use this alternating focus. The steady comparison or contrast of detail keeps the purpose of the paper more clearly and forcefully in the reader's mind.

Analogy

A special kind of comparison is the *analogy*, a comparison of two things that are unlike but that have similar attributes. The paragraph that developed the likeness between Lenin and Gladstone is a straight comparison: both belong to the same class. There is a resemblance between the men themselves. However, a comparison of death and sleep is an analogy: they are not similar states, but they have similar attributes — the cessation of activity and the appearance of repose.

Carefully used, the analogy can be instructive. Alexander Pope, an eighteenth-century English poet known for his wit, uses a brief analogy to emphasize a truth about human egoism:

> 'Tis with our judgments as our watches, none
> Go just alike, yet each believes his own.

The analogy is especially helpful in explaining the unfamiliar in terms of the familiar. For example, a lecturer in physiology in a class of teen-age boys might compare the heart with an automobile engine. Or a historian might compare the rise and fall of great civilizations with the life cycle of a human being. Thomas Huxley, a famous British biologist and defender of Charles Darwin's theory of evolution, uses analogy to enliven and clarify his idea that man needs to study the laws of nature in order to survive.

> Yet it is a very plain and elementary truth, that the life, the fortune and the happiness of every one of us, and, more or less, of those who are connected with us, do depend upon our knowing

something of the rules of a game infinitely more difficult and complicated than chess. It is a game which has been played for untold ages, every man and woman of us being one of the two players in a game of his or her own. The chessboard is the world, the pieces are the phenomena of the universe, the rules of the game are what we call the laws of Nature. The player on the other side is hidden from us. We know that his play is always fair, just, and patient. But also we know, to our cost, that he never overlooks a mistake, or makes the smallest allowance for ignorance. To the man who plays well, the highest stakes are paid, with that sort of overflowing generosity with which the strong shows delight in strength. And one who plays ill is checkmated—without haste, but without remorse. [From Thomas Henry Huxley, "A Liberal Education," *Macmillan's Magazine*, 1868.]

In the following paragraph George Orwell uses analogy to illustrate the character of England.

England is not the jewelled isle of Shakespeare's much quoted passage, nor is it the inferno depicted by Dr. Goebbels. More than either it resembles a family, a rather stuffy Victorian family, with not many black sheep in it but with all its cupboards bursting with skeletons. It has rich relations who have to be kow-towed to and poor relations who are horribly sat upon, and there is a deep conspiracy of silence about the source of the family income. It is a family in which the young are generally thwarted and most of the power is in the hands of irresponsible uncles and bedridden aunts. Still, it is a family. It has its private language and its common memories, and at the approach of an enemy it closes its ranks. A family with the wrong members in control—that, perhaps, is as near as one can come to describing England in a phrase. [From George Orwell, *My Country Right or Left 1940–1943*, Vol. II, *The Collected Essays, Journalism and Letters of George Orwell,* ed. Sonia Orwell and Ian Angus, Harcourt Brace Jovanovich, Inc., 1968, p. 68.]

An animal fable is a short narrative involving animals that act and talk like human beings from which a moral is drawn. A literary form that dates back hundreds of years, the fable is based on analogies between human beings and animals. Its primary purpose is to illustrate some human trait, to comment upon human behavior. In the following fable, entitled "The Shrike and the Chipmunks," James Thurber provides a humorous comment upon married life.

Once upon a time there were two chipmunks, a male and a female. The male chipmunk thought that arranging nuts in artistic patterns was more fun than just piling them up to see how many you could pile up. The female was all for piling up as many as you could. She told her husband that if he gave up making designs with the nuts there would be room in their large cave for a great many more and he would soon become the wealthiest chipmunk in the woods. But he would not let her interfere with his designs, so she flew into a rage and left him. "The shrike will get you," she said, "because you are helpless and cannot look after yourself." To be sure, the female chipmunk had not been gone three nights before the male had to dress for a banquet and could not find his studs or shirt or suspenders. So he couldn't go to the banquet, but that was just as well, because all the chipmunks who did go were attacked and killed by a weasel.

The next day the shrike began hanging around outside the chipmunk's cave, waiting to catch him. The shrike couldn't get in because the doorway was clogged up with soiled laundry and dirty dishes. "He will come out for a walk after breakfast and I will get him then," thought the shrike. But the chipmunk slept all day and did not get up and have breakfast until after dark. Then he came out for a breath of air before beginning work on a new design. The shrike swooped down to snatch up the chipmunk, but could not see very well on account of the dark, so he batted his head against an alder branch and was killed.

A few days later the female chipmunk returned and saw the awful mess the house was in. She went to the bed and shook her husband. "What would you do without me?" she demanded. "Just go on living, I guess," he said. "You wouldn't last five days," she told him. She swept the house and did the dishes and sent out the laundry, and then she made the chipmunk get up and wash and dress. "You can't be healthy if you lie in bed all day and never get any exercise," she told him. So she took him for a walk in the bright sunlight and they were both caught and killed by the shrike's brother, a shrike named Stoop.

Moral: Early to rise and early to bed makes a male healthy and wealthy and dead.

[From *Fables for Our Time*, published by Harper & Row. Originally printed in *The New York*. © 1940 James Thurber. © 1968 Helen Thurber.]

EXERCISE 7

Write a paragraph of 100 to 150 words on one of the topics listed below, and develop it by means of comparison or contrast. Decide on the bases of your comparison or contrast before you begin to write, and keep these bases in mind as you write. For example, if you plan to contrast two political leaders, you might contrast their origins, personalities, and political and philosophical attitudes. If you plan to compare two automobiles, you might want to compare their design, performance, economy, and comfort.

1. a comparison or contrast of two current political leaders, two popular entertainers, two types of students
2. a comparison or contrast between the attitudes of today's college-age generation and those of a preceding college-age generation on education, sexual behavior, race, dress, money, work, success
3. a contrast of the teaching styles of two instructors
4. a contrast of two views on capital punishment, welfare, off-shore drilling for oil, treatment of juvenile law breakers
5. a comparison or contrast of the rotary and piston engines
6. a short fable modeled after Thurber's "The Shrike and the Chipmunk"
7. an analogy between an investment counsellor and a college counsellor, running a university and running a business, position of women and position of blacks, responsibility of business corporation to the consumer and that of educational institution to the student, course of true love and a ship's passage over the ocean
8. an explanation of how Plato uses comparison, or more precisely analogy, in his description of the nature of reality (this information can be found in the first few pages of Book VII of the *Republic*)
9. a comparison or contrast of two friends, of a conservative and a liberal, a liberal and a radical, a conservative and a reactionary, a socialist and a communist
10. a contrast of two qualities—wit and humor, wisdom and intelligence, courage and rashness, training and education, ignorance and prejudice

4. ANALYSIS (DIVISION AND CLASSIFICATION)

Analysis is the process of dividing a subject into its component parts. It is an effective way of organizing material when the subject is rather complex. In using this process, the writer splits the subject into smaller parts in the topic sentence and then develops each part in turn, using any suitable method of development. In the following paragraph the writer uses descriptive detail and judgment to support the subordinate points.

There are three kinds of book owners. The first has all the

standard sets and best-sellers—unread, untouched. (This deluded individual owns woodpulp and ink, not books.) The second has a great many books—a few of them read through, most of them dipped into, but all of them as clean and shiny as the day they were bought. (This person would probably like to make books his own, but is restrained by a false respect for their physical appearance.) The third has a few books or many—everyone of them dog-eared and dilapidated, shaken and loosened by continual use, marked and scribbled in from front to back. (This man owns books.) [From Mortimer J. Adler, "How To Mark a Book," *Saturday Review,* July 6, 1940, p. 11.]

Topics that are easily separated into chronological, spatial, or structural components are especially suitable for analytic treatment. A chronological analysis divides on the basis of time. You would use this method if you were going to explain a process (tell how to make or do something) or analyze a historical event by dividing it into periods. In the following passage the writer explains how an Indian friend hunts.

Let me describe how a friend of mine from the Santo Domingo Pueblo hunts. He is twenty-seven years old. The Pueblo Indians, and I think probably most of the other Indians of the Southwest, begin their hunt, first, by purifying themselves. They take emetics, a sweat bath, and perhaps avoid their wife for a few days. They also try to think certain thoughts. They go out hunting in an attitude of humility. They make sure that they need to hunt, that they are not hunting without necessity. Then they improvise a song while they are in the mountains. They sing aloud or hum to themselves while they are walking along. It is a song to the deer, asking the deer to be willing to die for them. They usually still-hunt, taking a place alongside a trail. The feeling is that you are not hunting the deer, the deer is coming to you; you make yourself available for the deer that will present itself to you, that has given itself to you. Then you shoot it. After you shoot it, you cut the head off and place the head facing east. You sprinkle corn meal in front of the mouth of the deer, and you pray to the deer, asking it to forgive you for having killed it, to understand that we all need to eat, and to please make a good report to the other deer spirits that he has been treated well. One finds this way of handling things and animals in all primitive cultures. [From Gary Snyder, *Turtle Island.* Copyright © 1971 by Gary Snyder. Reprinted by permission of New Directions Publishing Corporation.]

The student who wrote the following paragraph analyzed Germany's military progress in the first year of the Second World War into three phases: the eastward thrust, the northern thrust, and the westward thrust.

During the first year of the Second World War, German military forces thrust first to the east, then to the north, and finally to the west. Successful in his attempt to regain the Sudetenland from Czechoslovakia, Hitler demanded that Poland give up the Polish Corridor and Danzig. When it became evident that Poland would not submit to his demand, German troops invaded Poland in September of 1939. German aircraft bombed and strafed Polish military formations and defenseless cities as well. Then mobile armored divisions drove through, encircled, and cut off enemy ground forces. After twenty-seven days Poland capitulated. In April of the following year, the German army occupied Denmark and Norway on the pretext that Britain and France were preparing to attack Russia, Germany's new ally, through the Scandinavian countries. On May 10, 1940, Germany's military juggernaut invaded the Netherlands and Belgium in its drive to conquer France. French defenses proved no match for Hitler's blitzkrieg tactics either, and on June 22, 1940, France was forced to sign an armistice with Germany.

The writer of this next paragraph analyzes a geographical area, the British Isles. This type of analysis is sometimes called a spatial analysis.

On the east, England is bounded by the North Sea, which is really nothing but an old depression which has gradually run full of water. Again a single glimpse at the map will tell you more than a thousand words. There on the right (the east) is France. Then we get something that looks like a trench across a road, the British Channel and the North Sea. Then the great central plain of England with London in the deepest hollow. Then the high mountains of Wales. Another depression, the Irish Sea, the great central Irish plain, the hills of Ireland, a few lonely rocks further toward the west, rearing their tops above the shallow sea. Finally the rock of St. Kilda (uninhabited since a year ago as it was too hard to reach) and then suddenly down we go, down, down, down, for there the real ocean begins and the last of the vast European Asiatic continent, both submerged and semi-submerged, here comes to an end. [From Hendrik Willem Van Loon, *Van Loon's Geography*. Reprinted by permission.]

A structural analysis divides a subject into its parts, types, elements, and shows how these subdivisions are related to each other to form a whole. The paragraph on page 60 that analyzes book owners is of this type. In the following paragraph, the writer analyzes the structure of an atom. (Note the use of analogy here also.)

The structure of atoms is like that of a minuscule solar system, with a heavy nucleus in the center as the sun, and much smaller bodies revolving around it as the planets. The nucleus is made up of two types of particles: protons, carrying a positive charge of electricity, and neutrons, electrically neutral. The planets revolving about the nucleus are electrons, units of negative electricity, which have a mass about one two-thousandths the mass of the proton or the neutron. The number of protons in the nucleus determines the chemical nature of the element, and also the number of planetary electrons, each proton being electrically balanced by an electron in the atom's outer shells. The total number of protons and neutrons in the nucleus is known as the mass number, which is very close to the atomic weight of the element, but not quite equal. Protons and neutrons are known under the common name "nucleons." [From William L. Laurence, *The Hell Bomb*, Alfred A. Knopf, 1951.]

These categories of analysis — chronological, spatial, and structural — are somewhat arbitrary. They overlap. The paragraph describing Germany's military moves in the Second World War, for example, contains a spatial as well as a chronological analysis; and the paragraphs on the British Isles could be considered a structural as well as a spatial analysis. Labels are not important here. What is important is that, whatever type of analysis you use, you make certain to show how the parts relate to each other and to the whole. Otherwise your analysis is apt to degenerate into a collection of facts without a central focus.

Here are some additional examples of paragraphs developed by analysis. In the first the writer uses definition and illustration to support his analysis.

The common varieties of bores are well known to everyone. Ambrose Bierce said that a bore is "a person who talks when you want him to listen," but as apt as the definition is, the species is a good deal more complicated than that. There are, for example, many gradations of boredom, such as the Crashing Bore whose conversation weighs on you like an actual physical burden that you want to throw off because it is stifling you, and quite a different kind, the Tinkling Bore whose conversation bothers you in the way that an insistent fly does, annoying but not dangerous. There are such types as the Still Waters Run Deep variety who defy you to say anything that will change the expression on their faces much less elicit an encouraging word from them. There you are on the sofa with them, their intense eyes peering at you with something between hopelessness and scorn, impressing on you the deep reservoir of their self-sufficiency and challenging you to ruffle the waters that lurk there. I cite this merely as an example of the passive as opposed to the militant type (both the Crashing and the Tinkling are militant), for it is those who make you feel like a bore who are the most boring of all. [From Russell Lynes, "Bores," in *Guests: Or How To Survive Hospitality*, p. 16. Copyright, 1951 by Harper & Row, Publishers, Inc. Reprinted by permission of Harper & Row, Publishers, Inc.]

In this next paragraph the writer uses examples to support his analysis.

Broadly speaking, invasions of privacy are of two sorts, both on the increase. There are those, like wiretapping, bugging and disclosure of supposedly confidential documents, that could conceivably be dealt with by changes in law or public policy. Then there are those that appear to be exercises of other rights—for example, freedom of speech, of the press, of inquiry. A newspaper reporter asks an impertinent personal question; the prospective employer of a friend wishes to know whether the friend has a happy sex life; a motivational researcher wishes to know what we have against Brand X deodorant; a magazine wishing to lure more advertisers asks us to fill out a questionnaire on our social, financial and intellectual status. Brandeis' "right to be let alone" is unique in that it can be denied us by the powerless as well as by the powerful—by a teen-ager with a protable radio as well as by a servant of the law armed with a subpoena. [From Richard H. Rovere, "Privacy and the Claims of Community," *The American Establishment and Other Reports, Opinions and Speculations*. © 1958, 1962 Harcourt Brace Jovanovich, Inc. By permission of author and publisher.]

EXERCISE 8

Write a paragraph of 100 to 150 words developing by analysis one of the following topics.

1. a chronological analysis of any of the following: a rock concert, souping up a stock car, an athletic event

2. varieties of sports fans, cigarette smokers, salesmen, automobile drivers, popular singers, contemporary lifestyles, comic strips, chauvinists, liberationists, motorcycle racers, joggers, loafers
3. types of teachers, weight watchers, bores, campus Romeos
4. operation of a solar power plant, geothermal power plant, fast breeder nuclear power plant, communication or weather satellite, laser beam, computer
5. the rotary internal-combustion engine, a steam turbine, a diesel engine, a modern windmill
6. classify students on one of the following bases: attitude toward studies, politics, the opposite sex, success, athletics
7. a limited geographical area—a stretch of beach, a mountain view, a desert scene, a campsite by a lake, a boulevard scene
8. an important battle of the Civil War, World War I or II (El Alamein, Guadalcanal, the Coral Sea, Bastogne)

5. DEFINITION

Students are frequently asked to define terms from a variety of disciplines: *capitalism, naturalism, symbolism, atomic fission, osmosis, plasticity,* and so forth. Learning to write clear definitions will therefore be of practical value to you. But more important, good definition promotes clear thinking and writing. Many disagreements would never have occurred if the disputants had taken care to define their terms adequately.

There are several ways to define. One is to use *examples,* illustrative instances:

An example of a marsupial is a wallaby.

This method is useful when writers can assume that readers know something of the meaning of the term: the examples simply provide further clarification. But when the reader lacks this knowledge, this method is rather confusing.

A second method defines by means of a *synonym,* a word with a similar meaning:

To denigrate means to defame, to sully, to disparage.
A roué is a rake, a debauchee.

This method is helpful if the synonym clarifies the original term, but not if the synonym is likely to be more abstract or general than the original term, as, for example:

Equivocal means ambiguous.

A third method, the *historical* or *etymological* method of definition, clarifies the meaning of a word by revealing its origin and the changes in meaning it has undergone. The following extract from *Webster's Third New International Dictionary* illustrates this type of definition.

Sinister . . . [Middle English *sinistre*, from the Latin *sinister* left, on the left side (whence Latin *sinistrum* evil, unlucky, inauspicious); from the fact that omens observed from one's left were considered unlucky] . . . (2) *obsolete:* conveying misleading or detrimental opinion or advice (the sinister application of the malicious, ignorant, and base intrepreter—Ben Jonson) . . . (4) evil or productive of evil: BAD, CORRUPTIVE (the sinister character of the early factory system—Walter Lippmann) . . . (5) . . . b. of ill omen by reason of being on the left side (the victor eagle, whose sinister flight retards our host—Alexander Pope) . . . [By permission. From *Webster's Third New International Dictionary*. Copyright 1966 by G. & C. Merriam Company, publishers of the Merriam-Webster Dictionaries.]

Another method, the *formal* definition, defines a term by placing it in a general class and then differentiating it from other members of the same class:

TERM		CLASS	DIFFERENTIATING DETAIL
A marsupial	*is*	an animal	that shelters its young in an external abdominal pouch containing mammary glands.
A hypothesis	*is*	an inference	that accounts, within the framework of a theory, for a set of facts and that can be used as the basis of action or further investigation.
Serendipity	*is*	the faculty	of stumbling upon fortunate, unexpected discoveries.

Defining analytically is an exacting process. You must observe several precautions to avoid inadequate and fallacious definitions:

1. The term to be defined should be specifically placed in a class. Statements that appear to be analytic definitions are sometimes simply descriptions of the object:

A steel mill is a noisy, smoky place with tall chimneys;

and sometimes they are interpretations of it:

Home is where the heart is.

In classifying an object, avoid using "is where" or "is when." *Where* signifies location, *when* signifies time, and neither represents a class of things:

ORIGINAL   Democracy is when the people rule themselves.
REVISION   Democracy is a form of government in which the people rule themselves.

2. The general class into which the term is placed should not be too extensive. Defining a telescope as something that helps the eye to see distant objects is not very helpful: the class of things is simply too broad. It could include, for example, binoculars, eyeglasses, magnifying glasses, and many others. In general, the narrower the classification, the clearer the definition. A telescope would thus be more precisely defined as an optical instrument, consisting of parts that fit and slide one within another, that enlarges the image of a distant object.

3. The definition should not repeat the name of the thing to be defined or a derivative of it:

Certified mail is mail that has been certified.

This definition still leaves the reader uninformed as to what "certified mail" means. Definitions that repeat the term to be defined, as in the example above, are called *circular* definitions, for they lead the reader back to where he started. A better definition would be:

Certified mail is first class mail for which proof of delivery is secured but for which no indemnity value is claimed.

4. The differentiation should be sufficient to distinguish the term clearly from other members of the class:

Buddhism is a religion of Asia.

This definition does not supply enough information to distinguish Buddhism from Mohammedanism, Hinduism, or Christianity, all religions of Asia. With the necessary information added, the meaning is clearer:

Buddhism is a religion of central and eastern Asia derived from the teachings of Gautama Buddha, who taught that suffering is inherent in life and that one can escape from it into *nirvana* — a state of spiritual peace — through mental and moral self-purification.

5. The definition should not be expressed in highly technical, obscure language. Dr. Samuel Johnson's definition of *network* as "anything reticulated or decussated, at equal distances with interstices between the intersections" is accurate but complex. The definition of *network* as a fabric or structure of threads, cords, or wires that cross each other at regular intervals and are knotted or secured at the crossings, as defined in *Webster's Third New International Dictionary,* is much simpler and clearer.

Observing these precautions will improve the clarity and precision of your formal definitions. There are times, however, when you will have to write more than a single sentence, a *minimum* definition, to define a term adequately. An explanation of Mohammedanism, freedom, or liberalism would obviously require more than one sentence. In developing a paragraph by means of definition, it is a good idea to start with a minimum definition as a basis and then use examples, comparisons, contrasts, historical information, and so forth, to support and extend your definition. Definitions that are developed in one or more paragraphs are called *extended* definitions.

The following paragraph offers a definition of the word *unconscious.*

The term "unconscious," now so familiar to all readers of modern works on psychology, gives offense to some adherents of the past. There should, however, be no special mystery about it. It is not a new animistic abstraction, but simply a collective word to include all the physiological changes which escape our notice, all the forgotten experiences and impressions of the past which continue to influence our desires and reflections and conduct, even if we cannot remember them. What we can remember at any time is indeed an infinitesimal part of what has happened to us. We could not remember anything unless we forgot almost everything. As Bergson says, the brain is the organ of forgetfulness as well as of memory. Moreover, we tend, of course, to become oblivious to things to which we are thoroughly accustomed, for habit blinds us to their existence. So the forgotten and the habitual make up a great part of the so-called "unconscious." [From "On Various Kinds of Thinking," from *The Mind in the Making* by James Harvey Robinson. Copyright 1921 by Harper & Brothers, renewed 1949 by Bankers

Trust Company. Reprinted by permission of Harper & Row, Publishers.]

Historian Arthur M. Schlesinger defines the terms *radical* and *conservative* in the paragraph below:

It should be clear, then, that the radical is a person who, in contrast to the conservative, favors a large participation of the people in the control of government and society and in the benefits accruing from such control. To attain his ideal the radical may become a protagonist of change; he usually has been one, as a matter of history, but this fact is a mere incident to, and not the touchstone of, his radicalism. The temperament of the radical is sanguine. He can say with Jefferson: "I steer my bark with Hope in the head, leaving fear astern. My hopes, indeed, sometimes fail; but not oftener than the forebodings of the gloomy." The conservative, on the other hand, is skeptical of the capacity of the mass of the people to protect their own interests intelligently; and believing that social progress in the past has always come from the leadership of wealth and ability, he is the consistent opponent of the unsettling plans of the radical. If the old saw is true that a pessimist is the wife of an optimist, perhaps the cynicism of the conservative is amply accounted for by his enforced association with the radical. The radical regards himself as a man of vision; but the conservative sees him only as a visionary. The radical as a type is likely to be broad-minded and shallow-minded; the disinterested conservative is inclined to be high-minded and narrow-minded. ["What Do the Terms Mean?" Reprinted with the permission of The Macmillan Company from *New Viewpoints in American History* by Arthur M. Schlesinger. Copyright 1922 by The Macmillan Company. Renewed 1950 by Arthur M. Schlesinger.]

In this paragraph Winston Churchill defines *civilization*. A minimum definition of the term is contained in the third sentence.

There are few words which are used more loosely than the word "Civilization." What does it mean? It means a society based upon the opinion of civilians. It means that violence, the rule of warriors and despotic chiefs, the conditions of camps and warfare, of riot and tyranny, give place to parliaments where laws are made, and independent courts of justice in which over long periods those laws are maintained. That is Civilization—and in its soil grow continually freedom, comfort and culture. When Civilization reigns in any country, a wider and less harassed life is afforded to the masses of people. The traditions of the past are cherished, and the inheritance bequeathed to us by former wise or valiant men becomes a rich estate to be enjoyed and used by all. [From Winston Churchill, *Blood, Sweat, and Tears,* G. P. Putnam's Sons, p. 45. Copyright 1941 by Winston S. Churchill.]

The authors of the following paragraph define the term *Renaissance* in its narrow and in its broader aspects. The first sentence provides a minimum definition of the term in its narrow sense, the fourth sentence in its broader aspect.

In a narrow sense, the Renaissance was a new and intense interest in the art and learning of Greece and Rome, to the disparagement of the Middle Ages. The Renaissance scholars, called humanists, imitated everything classical, loved the past, "were less interested in the present, and not at all in the future." This phase of the Renaissance was really regressive, for it looked backward in history toward antiquity. But the Renaissance in its broader aspects was a stimulation of interest in discoveries by explorers and scientists, a new urban culture of the rising middle class, new advances in statecraft and the growth of the national states, new concepts in literature and art, and a lively interest in secular affairs as contrasted with the other-worldliness of the Middle Ages. In its broad sense the Renaissance was progressive, for it looked forward in history and laid the foundations of our modern civilization. [From T. Walter Wallbank and Alastair M. Taylor, "What Was the Renaissance?" *Civilization: Past and Present,* 3rd ed., vol. 1, pp. 485–486, Scott, Foresman and Company, 1954.]

EXERCISE 9

A. In the blanks below indicate which of the following methods is used to define: (1) example, (2) synonym, or (3) formal. Write the number of your answer in the blank to the right of the sentence.

1. The snail, slug, oyster, and clam are examples of mollusks. _____

2. A palisade is a defensive barrier or fortification formed of pales. _____

3. Shakespeare's *As You Like It* is an example of romantic comedy. _____

4. A eulogy is a panegyric. _____

5. A ballad is a narrative poem, usually of folk origin and meant to be sung, consisting of simple stanzas and a recurrent refrain. _____

B. Some of the definitions given below violate the conditions necessary for a minimum formal definition. Mark the definitions as follows: (1) if the term has not been specifically placed in a class, (2) if the class into which the term has been placed is too large, (3) if the term is not sufficiently differentiated from other members of the same class, (4) if the term to be defined, or a derivative of it, is repeated in the definition, (5) if the definition is expressed in highly technical language, (6) if the definition seems clear and sound.

1. An *oligarchy* is a form of government in which the ruling power and influence is exercised by oligarchs. _____

2. *Pidgin* is the name of a mixed language, or jargon, developed by natives in the Orient and South Pacific for purposes of trade and incorporating the vocabulary of one or more languages with a simplified form of the grammatical system of one of these. _____

3. A monk is a man who seeks God. _____

4. A *pas de deux* is a ballet figure. _____

5. A hypochondriac is a person preoccupied with his or her imaginary ill health. _____

6. A bore is a person who speaks when you want him or her to listen. _____

7. A tachometer is a thing for measuring rotational speed. _____

8. A cheapskate is a person with short arms and low pockets. _____

9. An empiricist is one who believes in the primacy of empirical evidence. _____

10. A *raphe* is the part of the funiculus of an anatropous ovule adnate to the integument, forming a ridge along the body of the ovule that provides a diagnostic character in the various seeds. _____

C. Rewrite each of the following formal definitions in one sentence making
them more precise or more informative. Be prepared to explain why the
original version is inadequate.

1. A gourmet likes to eat well.

_____

_____

_____

2. Thor is one of the gods of Norse mythology.

_____

_____

_____

3. Burlesque is a form of comic mimicry.

_____

_____

_____

D. Reread the three paragraphs dealing with the terms *unconscious, radical*
and *conservative,* and *Renaissance* (pp. 68–70). For each definition list
(1) the *general class* into which the term has been placed and (2) the
differentiating detail that distinguishes the term from other members
of the class.

TERM	CLASS	DIFFERENTIATING DETAIL
1. The term "unconscious" *is*	_____	_____
		_____
		_____
2. A conservative *is*	_____	_____
		_____
		_____
3. The Renaissance *was*	_____	_____
		_____
		_____

E. Write an extended definition of any of the following terms. Begin with a minimum definition as your topic sentence and use illustration, comparison, contrast, or any other method of supporting topic sentences to develop your definition. Consult a dictionary, an encyclopedia, or any other reference work that will aid you, but write the definition in your own words.

1. a hypochondriac
2. a hypocrite
3. a neurotic or a psychotic
4. a bore or a boor
5. an idealist, a realist, or a fatalist
6. a liberal, a conservative, or a reactionary
7. a radical, a rebel, or a martyr
8. a connoisseur or a dilettante
9. a demagogue, civil disobedience
10. a patriot or a chauvinist
11. a humanist or a scientist
12. a successful person
13. a gourmet or a gourmand
14. an alcoholic
15. a communist or a socialist
16. wisdom or intelligence
17. an intellectual, a hippie, a hustler
18. a pacifist or a militarist
19. an amateur or a professional
20. a racist

6. COMBINATION OF METHODS

A good many, if not most, of the paragraphs you write will use a combination of the methods of paragraph development that have been explained and illustrated in this chapter. If you are developing a paragraph by means of examples, then statistics and other factual detail may strengthen your point. If your controlling idea requires definition for support, you will probably find comparison and contrast useful in providing additional clarification.

Here are two paragraphs that combine a variety of methods in their development. In the first, Albert Jay Nock discusses the meaning of education and training. He argues that education, unlike training, promotes dissatisfaction with the material rewards of life. In developing his point, he uses contrast, illustration, and judgmental observations.

Education, in a word, leads a person on to ask a great deal more from life than life, as at present organized, is willing to give him; and it begets dissatisfaction with the rewards that life holds out. Training tends to satisfy him with very moderate and simple returns. A good income, a home and family, the usual run of comforts and conveniences, diversions addressed only to the competitive or sporting spirit or else to raw sensation — training not only makes directly for getting these, but also for an inert and comfortable contentment with them. Well, these are all that our present society has to offer; so it is undeniably the best thing all round to keep people satisfied with them, which training does, and not to inject a subversive influence, like education, into this easy complacency. Politicians understand this — it is their business to understand it — and hence they hold up "a chicken in every pot and two cars in every garage" as a satisfying social ideal. But the mischief of education is its exorbitance. The educated lad may like stewed chicken and motor cars as well as anybody, but his education has bred a liking for other things too, things that the society around him does not care for and will not countenance. It has bred tastes which society resents as culpably luxurious and will not connive at gratifying. Paraphrasing the old saying, education sends him out to shift for himself with a champagne appetite amid a gin-guzzling society. [From Albert Jay Nock, "The Disadvantages of Being Educated," in *Free Speech and Plain Language* by Albert Jay Nock. Copyright 1937, William Morrow and Co., Inc.]

In the paragraph below the writer uses judgments, illustration, and contrast to develop his controlling idea.

If a democracy is to have any real meaning, it must respect the right of dissenters to resist the law in a nonviolent manner, so long as the dissenters are willing to face the legal consequences. Else, in time of war or other crisis, a democracy can turn as vicious as a tyranny. What is called the "positive law"—that is, the body of laws promulgated by a specific government—has no moral force unless it is grounded in the "natural." For instance, the laws against kulaks under Stalin, or against the Jews under Hitler, were inhuman perversions of the natural law, and deserved to be resisted, however "legal" they were. In such countries, "civil disobedience" was impossible—the dissenters would have been summarily executed—and therefore only revolutionary activity was effective. This is why only repressive governments have suffered revolution; they left no other way out for disagreement. [From "Rights and Limits of Dissent." From *Strictly Personal* by Sydney J. Harris. Reproduced through the courtesy of Field Newspaper Syndicate.]

EXERCISE 10

A. In the space provided indicate a suitable method of paragraph development for each of the following topic sentences:

1. At a rock concert one sees a variety of human types. _____

2. Inflation has been a serious problem for many nations in recent years.

   _____

3. Honesty is not invariably the best policy. _____

4. Planet Earth is like a spaceship. _____

5. Board surfing is an exciting sport. _____

6. The Martina X-9 Roadster is an expensive car to operate. _____

   _____

7. My European trip convinced me of the value of travellers' checks. _____

   _____

8. Three common types of college teachers are the sandbagger, the true believer, and the friendly philosopher. _____

9. Germany's military strategy during the first year of the Second World War included three phases: an eastward thrust, a northern thrust, and a westward thrust. _____

10. Intelligence is not the same thing as wisdom. _____

11. Japan's economy has made spectacular gains since the Second World War. _____

12. A successful teacher must be patient. _____

13. Liberty must be distinguished from license. _____

14. A free press is not always a responsible press. _____

15. Ultra Ferret was a clever detective. _____

16. One who obtains a college education secures several advantages in life.

    _____

17. The president of a university is like the chairman of the board of directors of a corporation. _____

18. Alcoholism is beginning to appear among teenagers today. _____

    _____

19. Juvenile crime has increased greatly within the past five years. _____

    _____

20. Hamlet and Abraham Lincoln had similar traits of character. _____

_____

B. For each of the six topics listed below, write five topic sentences that could be used as the basis of a paragraph.

1. the population explosion

_____

_____

_____

_____

_____

2. the automobile and air pollution

_____

_____

_____

_____

_____

3. the coming energy crisis in the United States

_____

_____

_____

_____

_____

4. medical care in the United States

_____

_____

_____

_____

_____

5. the institution of marriage in modern times

_____

_____

_____

_____

_____

6. truth in advertising

_____

_____

_____

_____

_____

C. Use the following sentences (and others you may wish to add) as supporting material for a paragraph on environmental pollution. Compose an appropriate topic sentence, and place it at the beginning of your paragraph.

1. Because of its durability, DDT retains its power to poison soil and bring about harmful changes in living tissue.
2. Hundreds of millions of years have been required to produce the plant and animal life now existing on the earth.
3. Strontium 90 is a dangerous chemical.
4. Rain washes DDT off plants and into the soil, rivers, lakes, and oceans, polluting water and killing fish.
5. Pollution of the air, water, and soil threatens life on earth.
6. If the insecticide DDT is sprayed on plants, it will enter the bodies of animals and humans eating these plants.
7. People must change their attitude toward nature: people are a part of nature, and to survive, they must not destroy their environment.
8. Chemicals in particular do serious damage to the ecological balance.
9. Strontium 90 can cause death in human beings by lodging in the bones and producing cancer.
10. Strontium is released into the air by nuclear explosions; it settles on plants and is absorbed into the earth.

79

D. Analyze the following paragraphs for completeness. Explain how those paragraphs you believe to be underdeveloped could be improved.

1. A student who works while attending college gains several economic, vocational, and social benefits. The economic benefits are obvious. In fact, a good number of students *must* work. They need money not only for tuition, texts, and lab fees but for basic living expenses: for food, clothing, rent, an automobile. For them work is not an option. If they don't work, they can't afford to go to school. But even for those students who are supported by their parents, a part-time job pays for dates, weekend trips, and various other luxuries that make college life less monotonous. And, finally, students who work gain vocational and social benefits as well.

2. The government should supervise the television industry more carefully. There are so many commercials on television today that viewers can hardly concentrate on the programs they are watching. And many of these commercials are misleading. Advertising money may keep television networks solvent, but it destroys the quality of entertainment they present.

3. But even when they listen, many young drug users tend to hear only what they want to hear. They talk about marijuana as a totally benign experience when, in truth, researchers still don't really know about its effects. Researchers have just gotten around to synthesizing its active ingredient, tetrahydro-cannabinol (THC). The conclusion so far, says Dr. Sidney Cohen, director of the National Institute of Mental Health's Division of Narcotic Addiction and Drug Abuse, is that "marijuana, taken infrequently and in small doses, causes no more difficulty than getting stoned on alcohol. But the question in everyone's mind is whether the pothead, the person who uses it consistently over a period of years, may suffer ill effects." Scientists are now trying to assess what some call the "amotivational syndrome" — whether marijuana can lead to a loss of ambition and drive. "I don't think one necessarily loses motivation if he is an occasional user," says Cohen, "but I suspect people who do make it a career do stop being interested in getting ahead, become more passive, tend to live only in the present and not to look to the future." [From "The Drug Generation: Growing Younger," *Newsweek*, April, 1969, p. 107. Copyright 1969 by Newsweek, Inc. All rights reserved. Reprinted by permission.]

4. The rising divorce statistics of recent years have prompted the suggestion that the traditional lifetime marriage contract be replaced by a short-term, renewable contract. This solution would, however, aggravate, not improve the situation, for it would create serious complications in the lives of the children of such a marriage and undermine the emotional relationship of the husband and wife. Those who support renewable, short-term marriages claim that traditional marriage ties are unrealistic because they seek to bind a couple together for life, a chancey proposition in a fast-moving world. But loosening those ties through short-term marriages will simply increase marital instability. In a successful marriage there must be time for the partners to adjust to each other's temperament. A short-term marriage decreases the chance of a

husband and wife's working out difficult problems by giving each partner an easy way out. Moreover, a happy marriage is not likely to result if one partner worries about whether the other will renew the contract.

5. Before buying a used car, you should inspect it carefully. Examine the engine first, for engine repairs can be costly and inconvenient. In checking the engine, look at the exhaust smoke. If it is blue, it may mean worn piston rings. Check the dip stick also. Heavy oil is sometimes used to make a mechanically defective engine run more smoothly. After examining the engine, inspect the body. Look for dents, scrapes, and rusted metal. Any body-repair cost should be added to the selling price. Open and close the doors to determine if the body is aligned. The frame of a car that has been in a serious accident may be bent out of shape; if this is the case, the doors may not hang or shut properly. A close scrutiny of the interior may also reveal evidence of the kind of care the car has received. Inexpensive seat covers may hide torn upholstery and broken springs. Next, consider the make and model of the car. Popular makes and models have a higher resale value. One more word of advice: if you know little about automobiles, take along a friend or a mechanic to advise you. Buying used cars involves some risk. If you want to get the most for your money in a used car, be alert and cautious.

E. As a preliminary suggestion to help you develop a paragraph by means of examples (p. 45), you were advised to work up a brief outline, transforming the topic into a specific topic sentence, jotting down details as they entered your mind, eliminating irrelevant items, and so forth. This procedure is helpful, for it demands that you think about your subject and get your thoughts in order before you begin to write, thus ensuring a more unified paragraph. Another useful technique, one proposed by Robert Louis Stevenson, involves imitation. Stevenson urged the young writer to imitate a variety of writing styles. Through such imitation, he argued, writers would gradually begin to develop a richer style of their own. One advantage of this method is that it offers writers a model, a standard for comparison — a decided asset to inexperienced writers, who, though they may have a fairly good idea of what to say, begin to flounder because they cannot find the right words, phrases, or sentences in which to express it.

After selecting a passage to imitate, Stevenson read the selection carefully, concentrating on its rhythm and structure. When he had fixed this movement and pattern in his mind, he selected an appropriate subject and tried to express his own thoughts in a similar style. Apply this procedure in this exercise. Read the model paragraph carefully, noting the placement of the topic sentence, the kinds of detail used to support the controlling idea, and the wording and sentence structure. Then choose one of the topics listed and compose your own paragraph, imitating the general pattern and style of the model.

The topic sentence in this paragraph is the first sentence. The second sentence comments on the controlling idea in the topic sentence — capital punishment should be abolished — and informs the reader that the primary detail will consist of reasons. Sentences 3, 7, 9, and 10 supply these reasons. Sentences 4, 5, 6, 8, 11, 12, and 13 provide secondary support. You need not try to imitate the exact structure or wording of each sentence, but copy the general plan of the paragraph and use expressions such as "in recent years," "for one thing," "another argument," "it is also argued," and "but perhaps the most appealing argument" to introduce your reasons. Round off your paragraph with an appropriate quotation.

(1) *In recent years* an increasing number of Americans have become convinced that capital punishment should be abolished. (2) This conviction may appear to be a sentimental evasion of the harsh reality of increasing criminal violence in this country, *but reasons for this attitude are not hard to find.* (3) *For one thing*, executing a murderer does not deter others from committing murder. (4) States that have prohibited the death penalty — Michigan, Maine, Iowa, Minnesota, to name a few — have not experienced a significant increase in their murder rate. (5) Nor was this the case in eighteenth-century England when many crimes, including pickpocketing, were punishable by death; and public hangings were held to emphasize the point. (6) People gathered to witness the hanging often had their pockets picked by skilled thieves undeterred by the threat of the noose tightening around their own necks. (7) *Another argument* frequently raised against capital punishment is that it involves an appalling risk. (8) Since judges, juries, and prosecuting attorneys are not infallible, an innocent person may be executed. (9) *It is also argued* that legal execution is a primitive, discredited idea rooted in revenge and retribution. (10) *But perhaps the most appealing argument* is that it violates the sanctity of human life. (11) It is a negative, life-denying symbol of man's inhumanity to man. (12) Albert Camus, the French Nobel Laureate, writes, "The man of today wants laws and institutions suitable to a convalescent, which will curb him and lead him without crushing him. . . . The death penalty," he adds, ". . . is a revolting butchery, an outrage inflicted on the person and body of man." [From "Reflections on the Guillotine," Albert Camus.]

TOPICS
1. a police officer's, firefighter's, or doctor's right to strike
2. better treatment for blacks, Spanish-speaking people, or American Indians
3. short-term, renewable marriage contracts
4. offshore drilling for oil
5. euthanasia
6. the United Nations as a world forum
7. plea bargaining
8. extending the territorial boundary of the United States 200 miles out to sea
9. a favorite recreational activity — for instance car racing, surfing, skiing, scuba diving
10. popularity of sports cars, vans, motorcycles, campers, mobile homes
11. reducing American consumption of beef to conserve feed grains for shipment to hungry nations abroad

SUMMARY

Good paragraphs must be adequately developed. You should therefore take special care to see that your paragraphs contain sufficient supporting material to explain clearly and fully your topic statement. There are a number of ways to do this: (1) use *illustrative detail* — examples, illustrations, anecdotes — when you can clarify by pointing to a particular incident, a concrete phenomenon; (2) use *facts* and *statistics* when verifiable detail is required to substantiate your point; (3) use *comparison* and *contrast* if you explain your subject best by noting how it is similar to or different from another object or situation; (4) use *analysis* if your subject lends itself naturally to subdivision; (5) use *definition* when your purpose requires the establishment of the meaning of a term; and (6) use a *combination* of any of these methods whenever you need or desire a variety of supporting material.

CHAPTER THREE | Coherence

Clear, readable paragraphs must be coherent as well as unified and well developed. Their sentences must not only adequately develop a controlling idea but they also must link together smoothly. Each sentence should lead into the next so that the reader can easily follow the progression of thought. To achieve this orderly progression, you must arrange your material in some logical sequence and provide connecting links between sentences.

To help your reader understand your meaning quickly and easily, you must take special care with this first task, the proper ordering of ideas. In the following paragraph, for example, the lack of an orderly grouping of the sentences disrupts the continuity.

(1) The yes man had no place in the pioneer tradition. (2) The pioneer had his faults and his virtues. (3) The virtues included a sturdy independence, and the compulsion, if need arose, to look every man level in the eye and tell him to go to hell. (4) Reasonably secure in the fruits of his own labor and thus economically independent, he could express in any company his honest opinion as forcibly as he pleased, and, subject to the local *mores* — the base line from which all human behavior must stem — he could translate his beliefs into tangible performance. (5) The faults included a prodigal wastefulness, a disposition to befoul one nest and move on to the next, a certain laxity in respect to the social amenities. (6) His opinions may have been frequently deplorable, his acts often crude and peremptory, but he was free to be true to the bent that he knew — and so, by the Eternal! a man, and not a rubber stamp. (7) He could vote for candidates he respected, agitate for reforms he believed in, refuse to do jobs which galled his sense of

decency or craftsmanship, come and go as the seasons dictated, but not at the bidding of any overlord.

This paragraph contains enough detail to support its controlling idea, but it lacks an orderly progression. The first two sentences convey its controlling idea: although pioneers had faults to balance virtues, they were no yes men. The second sentence, by mentioning faults first, leads the reader to expect the writer to deal first with them. The third sentence, however, begins with virtues. The fourth sentence continues the discussion of virtues. In the fifth sentence the focus shifts to the pioneer's faults. But in the sixth and seventh sentences the focus shifts back to virtues. The paragraph would have been more coherent and hence less confusing if all the details concerning faults had been presented first and those concerning virtues second. The intention of the paragraph is clearly to emphasize the virtues of the pioneer (four sentences concern virtues; only one concerns faults), yet the fifth sentence confuses the organization of the detail and so diffuses the force of the paragraph. The sixth sentence, furthermore, should conclude the paragraph, for it summarizes the dominant idea, and it contains the strongest emotional force of any sentence.

Notice how much more coherent the paragraph becomes when the same sentences are grouped more logically. The paragraph now appears as Stuart Chase composed it.

The yes man had no place in the pioneer tradition. The pioneer had his faults and his virtues. The faults included a prodigal wastefulness, a disposition to befoul one nest and move on to the next, a certain laxity in respect to the social amenities. The virtues included a sturdy independence, and the compulsion, if need arose, to look every man in the eye and tell him to go to hell. Reasonably secure in the fruits of his own labor and thus economically independent, he could express in any company his honest opinions as forcibly as he pleased, and, subject to the local *mores* — the base line from which all human behavior must stem — he could translate his beliefs into tangible performance. He could vote for candidates he respected, agitate for reforms he believed in, refuse to do jobs which galled his sense of decency or craftsmanship, come and go as the seasons dictated, but not at the bidding of any overlord. His opinions may have been frequently deplorable, his acts often crude and peremptory, but he was free to be true to the best that he knew — and so, by the Eternal! a man, and not a rubber stamp. [From Stuart Chase, "The Luxury of Integrity," *The Nemesis of American Business*, The Macmillan Co. Copyright 1931, p. 30.]

ORDERING IDEAS

If your paragraphs are to be coherent, you must first arrange your materials in a logical order. The kind of order you use will depend on your purpose and the nature of your materials. When you wish to narrate a sequence of events or present the steps of a process, you should use a *narrative order,* arranging the detail on the basis of time. When you wish to describe something—a landscape, a person, the structure of an atom—you should use a *descriptive order,* organizing the detail in terms of spatial relationships. And when you wish to explain an idea, you should use an *expository order,* grouping the detail in the most effective sequence to support and clarify your idea. These three categories are somewhat arbitrary—the controlling idea of an expository paragraph, for example, may be developed by means of a spatial or process analysis—but they do provide a convenient illustration of common patterns of ordering sentences in a paragraph. In the discussion that follows we shall explain and illustrate these three methods in greater detail.

Narrative Order

Arranging the detail of a paragraph in chronological order is a natural and effective method of describing a historical event. The writer of the following paragraph groups his detail in this manner as he briefly reconstructs Grant's attack on Vicksburg during the Civil War.

Meanwhile the fighting resumed. In the west Grant began an investment of Vicksburg. He moved south from Memphis, made camp on the west bank of the river, and felt out possible approaches through the swampy jungle athwart the mouth of the Yazoo. Its impracticability turned him to the more audacious strategy of a sweep around the Confederate rear to attack Vicksburg's weaker exposure on the south and east. Preparatory to this move he sent a cavalry force on a still wider encirclement to burn bridges and tear up tracks leading toward Vicksburg. Then with some twenty thousand men he marched south, rendezvoused with the Union flotilla for a recrossing of the Mississippi, and swung east, north, and west toward his target. En route he had to fight five pitched battles with Pemberton's men from Vicksburg and Johnston's from Chattanooga. In these engagements he took ten thousand prisoners and drove the remainder of Pemberton's men back into Vicksburg. Two attempts to carry the fortification by assault failed, but siege and bombardment succeeded. On July 4 Pemberton and his command of some thirty thousand men surrendered. Capture of Fort Hudson soon followed, and the Mississippi was securely in Union hands. The strategy of driving a wedge through the Confederacy along the all-important Mississippi had been achieved. [From John W. Caughey and Ernest R. May, *A History of the United States,* © 1964 by Rand McNally and Company, Chicago, p. 253. Reprinted by permission of Rand McNally College Publishing Company.]

Descriptive Order

The details in a descriptive paragraph are arranged to give the reader a clear picture of the object described. In the following paragraph Ted Morgan describes the view of Rio de Janeiro from atop Corcovado Mountain, first on his right, then directly ahead of him, and then to his left.

Rio today has the strangest urban layout of any city I have seen. It is a combination of great city and year-round summer resort, as if Acapulco had been grafted onto Manhattan. Grasping its shape requires a climb to the top of Corcovado (hunchbacked) Mountain, where one stands in the shadow of a graceless, thousand-ton concrete Christ with outstretched arms. Two thousand, three hundred feet below, the scalloped coastline unfolds — to the right, the long strip of white Atlantic beach, the broad sidewalk of gray and black granite chips (called "Portuguese stone") in wave-like patterns and the sweeping, symmetrical line of twelve-story apartment buildings and hotels, now unfortunately broken by skyscrapers. Directly ahead, the bay's bottleneck entrance and Sugarloaf Mountain, and to the left, the polluted bay beaches, the harbor dotted with ships, gardens tufted with royal palms, and the downtown area, which meanders through the gaps between the steep, uninhabited cones. To get from the sea side to the bay side one must tunnel under the mountains, one reason this city of five million has such a traffic problem. The paradox of Rio is that it is a mythical destination like Capri and Tahiti, whose very name is a promise of pleasure, but at the same time it has the seemingly insoluble problems of a big city. [From Ted Morgan, "Brazil!" *Travel and Leisure,* October, 1975, p. 32. Copyright © 1975 American Express Publishing Company. Reprinted by permission of Brandt & Brandt.]

Expository Order

Expository order includes a number of grouping patterns. The most frequently used are the *inductive,* the *deductive,* and the *climactic.*

Induction is a process of reasoning in which one proceeds from an examination of particular facts to the formulation of a conclusion that accounts for these facts. An inductive paragraph often ends with its topic sentence. When writers think their readers may resist the point they wish to make, they often use an inductive order to present their facts, illustrations, and definitions before their conclusion.

In the paragraph below Edith Hamilton reserves her main point — that tragedy should only be used to describe the suffering of a soul that can suffer greatly — for the last sentence, after she has presented the concrete detail that illustrates it.

One dark page of Roman history tells of a little seven-year-old girl, daughter of a man judged guilty of death and so herself condemned to die, and how she passed through the staring crowds sobbing and asking, "What had she done wrong? If they would tell her, she would never do it again" — and so on to the black prison and the executioner. That breaks the heart, but it is not tragedy, it is pathos. No heights are there for the soul to mount to, but only the dark depths where there are tears for things. Undeserved suffering is not in itself tragic. Death is not tragic in itself, not the death of the beautiful and the young, the lovely and beloved. Death felt and suffered as Macbeth feels and suffers is tragic. Death felt as Lear feels Cordelia's death is tragic. Ophelia's death is not a tragedy. She being what she is, it could be so only if Hamlet's and Laertes' grief were tragic grief. The conflicting claims of the law of God and the law of man are not what makes the tragedy of the *Antigone*. It is Antigone herself, so great, so tortured. Hamlet's hesitation to kill his uncle is not tragic. The tragedy is his power to feel. Change all the circumstances of the drama and Hamlet in the grip of any calamity would be tragic, just as Polonius would never be, however awful the catastrophe. The suffering of a soul that can suffer greatly — that and only that is a tragedy. [Reprinted from *The Greek Way* by Edith Hamilton. By permission of W. W. Norton & Company, Inc. Copyright 1930, 1943 by W. W. Norton & Company, Inc. Copyright renewed 1958, 1971.]

Deduction is a process of reasoning that proceeds from a generalization to a conclusion derived from that generalization. A paragraph in which the materials have been arranged deductively thus begins with the topic statement followed by the detail in support of this statement. The following paragraph illustrates the deductive order of development:

Expressing one's thoughts is one skill that the school can really teach, especially to people born without natural writing or speaking talent. Many other skills can be learned later—in this country there are literally thousands of places that offer training to adult people at work. But the foundations for skill in expression have to be laid early: an interest in and an ear for language; experience in organizing ideas and data, in brushing aside the irrelevant, in wedding outward form and inner content into one structure; and above all, the habit of verbal expression. If you do not lay these foundations during your school years, you may never have an opportunity again. [From Peter Drucker, "How to Be an Employee," *Fortune,* May, 1952, p. 127. Reprinted courtesy of *Fortune.*]

Readers are apt to remember best what they read last. Therefore, writers frequently organize their detail in an order of climax, beginning with the least important detail and closing with the most important. This pattern is effective when one of the facts, examples, or judgments used to develop a paragraph is especially relevant and impressive. In the following sentences the ideas are arranged in an order of climax:

1. In 1923 Henry Merritt became a full professor, published his first book, and won a Pulitzer Prize.
2. Last Thursday I had a frustrating day: I slept through my eight o'clock class, failed a test in biology, and smashed my car against a telephone pole.
3. The cashmere sport coat was well-tailored and good looking, but far too expensive for me.

The paragraph below is arranged in an order of climax:

A work of literature may be studied in relation to its author, to the culture from which it springs, and to the text itself. One may study a writer's work for the information it gives about the character of the writer or about his or her world view. A reader must be careful, however, in drawing inferences about a person from his or her writings: the attitudes and values of the hero of a novel do not necessarily reflect those of the author. Because a literary work is a product of an age, a knowledge of the political and economic conditions and the philosophic and religious ideas of that age is useful. A knowledge of Dante's theological views, for example, helps the student to better understand the *Divine Comedy.* But however interesting and helpful, concern for the author or the author's background is essentially secondary. The study of the work itself is primary. If we are to get at the heart of a novel, a play, or a poem, we must focus on its content and structure. We must concern ourselves with the experience—the ideas and attitudes—the author communicates and the form in which he or she communicates it.

Three other possibilities for the ordering of detail in an expository paragraph are the orders of *familiarity, complexity,* and *cause and effect.* Writers attempting to explain a difficult subject frequently arrange detail in an order of familiarity, proceeding from the known to the unknown. For example, if a writer were explaining the principle of jet propulsion, he or she might begin with a reference to the flight of a balloon from which the air had suddenly been released. In the order of complexity simpler details are presented first and are followed by more complicated ones. And in the order of cause and effect, the writer organizes the material to trace the relationship between a cause and its resulting effect. The cause-and-effect order is quite similar to the narrative order, but it has a causal rather than a chronological emphasis.

EXERCISE 11

A. The sentences in the following paragraphs have been scrambled so that they are improperly ordered. Rearrange the sentences to form a more coherent paragraph and indicate the new order by writing the numbers of the sentences in their proper sequence in the blanks following each paragraph. Indicate also the type of order each writer has used: *narrative*, *descriptive*, or *expository*.

1. (1) There is no clue as to where and when to stop. (2) For all the geologist can tell, the earth may have existed forever. (3) How long has the surface of the earth been washing away in this fashion? (4) A plateau two miles high is removed in 100 million years. (5) Because this thickness of material has been worn away and replaced several times in some parts of the globe, it follows that the earth must be at least several hundred million years old. (6) Moreover, the ceaseless cycle of erosion and uplifting has been going on as far back into history, and as deep into the crust of the earth, as we are able to see. (7) We can measure the amount of material which is removed each year from the American continent, for example, by the major rivers such as the Mississippi. (8) It is estimated that 800 million tons of soil are washed away to the sea from the continental United States in a year. (9) At this rate the level of the land is lowered by one foot in 10,000 years. . . . [From p. 123 (rearranged) in *Red Giants and White Dwarfs*, Rev. Ed., by Robert Jastrow. Copyright © 1967, 1971 by Robert Jastrow. Reprinted by permission of Harper & Row, Publishers, Inc.]

Proper Sequence _____

Type of Order _____

2. (1) Another non-racing vehicle, however, proved to be one of the most popular entries in the show. (2) But the classics of the 30's hold little appeal for the young drivers of the 70's, and during the day the yellow roadster often seemed forlorn and ignored by the crowds of students. (3) From the carpeted floor, grained plywood panels rose to an acoustical ceiling of suspended cork tiles, and eight speakers filled the interior with stereo sound from a tape recorder mounted under the dash and equipped with remote controls. (4) It was a bright orange 1969 Dodge van, and all day clusters of observers peered into the dark cavern between its rear doors. (5) Inside they found a pillow-and-stereo-finished pad, completely equipped for rocking out. (6) Another tape deck stood in the van itself; it wasn't clear whether it was an integral part of the system or just an auxiliary. (7) A psychedelic sound light flashed and throbbed with the pulse of the music, and for really solid comfort there was a small portable liquor cabinet—the bottles all empty, however, in deference to campus rules. (8) One could lie back on the huge pillows concealing the engine housing, tune, turn, and drop off to sleep—after switching on the ultraviolet light for a last look at the psychedelic posters. [From James

Armstrong, "Class and Comfort at the Auto Show," *The Faculty Focus,* Vol. 8, Issue 4, Fullerton Junior College, May, 1969.]

Proper Sequence _____

Type of Order _____

3. (1) It is so important, in fact, that Americans who do not or cannot read well today are severely handicapped in their ability to participate effectively in the common activities and enterprises of American life. (2) In the last three hundred years reading has become an increasingly important means of achieving respect for the individual. (3) For the waves of immigrants who washed across America in the nineteenth century the ability to read became the most important responsibility of new citizens as they sought to absorb the common culture of their new land. (4) The Puritans who settled in New England in the seventeenth century encouraged their followers to read the Bible, and Bible reading became a major influence in the development of schools in the Colonial period. (5) During the Reformation in the sixteenth century, reading was elevated in importance because it was considered necessary for the individual to read and interpret the Bible for himself. (6) Today reading is even more important as an increasing flood of printed matter rolls off the presses and the printed word has been reinforced by the power of the spoken word on radio and television.

Proper Sequence _____

Type of Order _____

B. Leaf through a magazine, newspaper, or book to find an example of a paragraph organized in each of the following patterns: (1) narrative, (2) descriptive, and (3) expository. Be prepared to explain which of the various types of expository order is used in the paragraph arranged in an expository order.

C. Using a climactic order, write a paragraph of 100 to 125 words on one of the following subjects:

  1. a disastrous experience
  2. the transition from high school to college
  3. violence in modern professional sports
  4. the unrestricted sale of firearms
  5. cost of malpractice insurance for doctors
  6. child abuse in the United States
  7. the problem of waste disposal in the United States
  8. protecting American fish stocks against depletion by foreign fishing fleets
  9. terrorism as means of achieving political goals
  10. living conditions for children of migrant farm workers

D. Select an interesting object, scene, or person and write a paragraph of 100 to 125 words describing your subject. Focus on one or two prominent features. Select significant detail. Do not attempt a complete rendering.

DEVICES FOR ENSURING COHERENCE

Coherence in a paragraph depends basically on an orderly arrangement of ideas. If readers cannot follow the direction of thought, they are apt to become confused and puzzled, to feel that the parts of the paragraph do not cohere. But incoherence is not solely a matter of logical sequence. It depends also on the use of explicit connecting links between sentences. Consider, for example, the following adaptation of a paragraph about one of the most successful creations of the motion picture industry — the Western hero.

> The Western hero is a figure of repose. He resembles the gangster in being lonely and to some degree melancholy. His melancholy comes from the "simple" recognition that life is unavoidably serious, not from the disproportions of his own temperament. His loneliness is organic, not imposed on him by his situation but belonging to him intimately and testifying to his completeness. The gangster must reject others violently or draw them violently to him. The Westerner is not compelled to seek love; he is prepared to accept it. He never asks of it more than it can give. We see him constantly in situations where love is at best an irrelevance. If there is a woman he loves, she is usually unable to understand his motives; she is against killing and being killed; he finds it impossible to explain to her that there is no point in being "against" these things: they belong to his world.

The continuity of thought in this paragraph is obstructed by the lack of explicit connecting links between sentences. As a result, the writer's thought does not flow as smoothly from sentence to sentence. When the links are provided, notice how much more coherent the paragraph becomes, how much clearer the contrast between the gangster and the Westerner.

> The Western hero, *by contrast,* is a figure of repose. He resembles the gangster in being lonely and to some degree melancholy. *But* his melancholy comes from the "simple" recognition that life is unavoidably serious, not from the disproportions of his own temperament. *And* his loneliness is organic, not imposed on him by his situation but belonging to him intimately and testifying to his completeness. The gangster must reject others violently or draw

them violently to him. The Westerner is not *thus* compelled to seek love; he is prepared to accept it, *perhaps, but* he never asks of it more than it can give, *and* we see him constantly in situations where love is at best an irrelevance. If there is a woman he loves, she is usually unable to understand his motives; she is against killing and being killed, *and* he finds it impossible to explain to her that there is no point in being "against" these things: they belong to his world. [From Robert Warshow, "The Westerner," *The Immediate Experience,* Doubleday & Co., 1954.]

Transitional Words and Phrases

The words and phrases italicized in the paragraph above act as bridges between the sentences. *By contrast, but, thus,* and similar expressions provide transitions between sentences to make it easier for the reader to follow the writer's thought. Although overuse of such expressions as *therefore, however,* and *in the last analysis* can make writing awkward and mechanical, used moderately and with variety they can improve paragraph coherence. Beginning writers should try to develop skill in the use of these expressions.

Some words and phrases commonly used to provide continuity between sentences, or within the sentence itself, are listed below.

Relationship	*Expression*
addition, sequence	and, also, in addition, moreover, furthermore, first, second, again
contrast	but, however, nevertheless, notwithstanding, on the other hand, yet, still
similarity	similarly, likewise, in a like manner, in the same way, in a similar case
exemplification, illustration	for example, as an illustration, for instance, as an example
restatement, clarification	in other words, that is, in particular, in simpler terms
concession	though, although, even though, granted that, it may be true that
emphasis	most important, indeed, in fact, I repeat, certainly, truly, admittedly
conclusion, result	therefore, consequently, thus, as a consequence, hence, as a result
summation	to sum up, in conclusion, finally, in short, in sum, in summary

Repetition of Key Terms

The repetition of key words and phrases provides another way to connect sentences within a paragraph. The deliberate repetition of words that carry the basic meaning emphasizes them in the reader's mind and thus serves to weave together the sentences that contain them. Students are frequently advised to avoid repeating words, and such advice is often valid. The frequent recurrence of unimportant words can make writing mechanical and monotonous, thus dulling reader interest. But do not be afraid to repeat important words to explain your thought clearly. A haphazard use of synonyms for the sake of variety may simply confuse your reader and defeat your purpose.

The paragraph below provides a pattern of linkage through the repetition of such words as *Japanese, company, employee*.

As a result, the *Japanese* worker usually feels a deep loyalty to his firm, which almost always employs him until he retires or dies. Working for the advancement of the *company* is elevated into a life goal for the worker. *Japanese* society encourages this by identifying a man not by his profession, but by the *company* he works for. "If you ask a man what he does," says one *Japanese* businessman, "he will say he is with Mitsubishi regardless of whether he is a driver or vice president." Often a *Japanese employee's* life revolves more around his *company* than his family. A 1971 government poll revealed that almost one-third of *Japanese employees* felt that work was the most meaningful part of their lives. [From "The Japanese Yen for Work," *Newsweek,* March 26, 1973, p. 82. Copyright Newsweek, Inc. 1973, reprinted by permission.]

In the following paragraph the writer ties his sentences together through a repetition of the words *thinking, thought, writing, written,* and *words*.

It is surely no accident that greater lucidity and accuracy in *thinking* should result from the study of clarity and precision in *writing*. For *writing* necessarily uses *words,* and almost all *thinking* is done with *words*. One cannot even decide what to have for dinner, or whether to cross town by bus or taxi, without expressing the alternatives to oneself in *words*. My experience is, and the point of my whole course is, that the discipline of marshaling *words* into formal sentences, *writing* them down, and examining the *written* statement is bound to clarify *thought*. Once ideas have been *written* down, they can be analyzed critically and dispassionately; they can be examined at another time, in another mood, by another expert. *Thoughts* can therefore be developed, and if they are not precise at the first *written* formulation, they can be made so at a second attempt. [From F. Peter Woodford, "Sounder Thinking Through Clearer Writing," *Science,* Vol. 156, May 12, 1967, pp. 743–45. Copyright 1967 by the American Association for the Advancement of Science.]

Parallelism

A third way to ensure continuity within a paragraph is to phrase important ideas in the same grammatical structures. The recurrence of similar grammatical forms and the consequent repetition of rhythmic patterns tends to make writing concise, emphatic, and easy to follow. Recurring patterns of expression are effective in speech as well as writing, as the first example below illustrates. The parallel repetitions in each passage have been italicized.

1. "that this nation, under God, shall have a new birth of free-dom; and that government *of the people, by the people, for the people,* shall not perish from the earth." [From Abraham Lincoln's "Gettysburg Address."]

2. "Reading maketh *a full man;* conference *a ready man;* and writing *an exact man.* And therefore, *if* a man *write little, he had need have a great memory; if he confer little, he had need have a present wit;* and *if he read little, he had need have much cunning.*" [From Francis Bacon, "Of Studies."]

3. "We hold these truths to be self-evident, *that* all men *are created* equal, *that* they *are endowed* by their Creator with certain unalienable rights, *that* among these *are life, liberty* and the *pursuit* of happiness." [From the Declaration of Independence.]

Winston Churchill uses parallel repetition to structure his thought and give balance and coherence to his description of Leon Trotsky.

But he must have been a difficult man to please. *He did not like* the Czar, *so he murdered* him and his family. *He did not like* the Imperial Government, *so he blew* it up. *He did not like* the Liberalism of Guchkov and Miliukov, *so he overthrew* them. *He could not endure* the Social Revolutionary moderation of Kerensky and Savinkov, *so he seized* their places. And *when at last the Com-*

munist regime for which he had striven with might and main *was established* throughout the whole of Russia, *when the Dictatorship of the Proletariat was supreme, when the New Order of Society had passed from visions into reality, when the hateful culture and traditions of the individualist period had been eradicated, when the Secret Police had become the servants of the Third International, when* in a word *his Utopia had been achieved, he* was still discontented. *He* still *fumed, growled, snarled, bit* and *plotted.* . . . [From Winston Churchill, *Great Contemporaries*, G. P. Putnam's Sons, New York, 1937, pp. 167–68. Reprinted by permission of The Hamlyn Publishing Group, Ltd.]

In the next paragraph the writer uses parallel repetition to stress her point that "untutored teen-age consumers bear a large share of responsibility in elevating the punk."

Some say that religion no longer plays a vital role in setting standards, that we may pay it lip service but no heed. *Some say that parents no longer* pass on to their children a clear code of ethics. *Some blame* the school for not providing what the home neglects, and here I think a legitimate question can be raised concerning one particular aspect of education: the standards of craftsmanship. If the young were taught the basic requirements of a good job, they would be more critical of *the singer without a voice, the star without talent.* Untutored teen-age consumers bear a large share of responsibility in elevating the punk. It is *their money that buys the records* of the bad singer, *their ecstatic squeals that sustain* him, *their tastes that too many of the mass media cater to.* [From Marya Mannes, "Let's Stop Exalting Punks." Reprinted with permission from the January 1963 *Reader's Digest*, p. 47. Copyright 1962 by The Reader's Digest Association, Inc. Condensed from *The Saturday Evening Post.*]

Pronoun Reference

Another way to establish continuity between sentences is through the use of pronouns. Using a pronoun in one sentence to repeat a noun in a previous sentence provides an effective link between these sentences. In the following paragraph, lines have been drawn connecting pronouns with their antecedents to indicate graphically how the reader's attention is naturally directed back to the antecedent of a pronoun. This repetition of key words through the use of pronouns ties these sentences together.

To be dissatisfied when you are young with the way you are taught is both necessary and honorable. Flawless teaching would be ineffectual in forming a man; if the child is to attain his full adult stature, he needs to be treated adeptly—but ineptly, too. The vice of rigidly systematic education is that it can produce only a child-man, which happened to many young princes in the past and perhaps even to Jean Jacques Rousseau's Emile. So thank heaven that your early teachers have defects and inadequacies, for otherwise you would have nothing to react against. Conflict is an essential first-hand experience. A teacher instructs you by what he gives you, yes, but he also stimulates you by his very deficiencies; he pushes you on to becoming your own inner teacher. [From p. 1 Jean Guitton, *A Student's Guide to Intellectual Work*, Trans. Adrienne Foulke, University of Notre Dame Press, 1964. Reprinted by permission.]

In the next example the writer repeats *he* and *his* to carry his thought throughout the paragraph.

Just under three hundred years ago, the Lucasian Professor of Mathematics at Cambridge did a distinctly unusual thing. *He* decided that one of *his* pupils was a much better mathematician than *he* was, and in all respects more fitted for *his* job. *He* wasn't content with this exercise in self-criticism. *He* promptly resigned *his* Chair, on condition that *his* pupil be immediately appointed. In the light of history, no one can say that *his* judgment was wrong. For the Professor's name was Barrow, and *he* was a very good mathematician by seventeenth-century standards; but *his* pupil was Isaac Newton. [From C. P. Snow, "On Magnanimity," *Harper's Magazine*, July, 1962, p. 37.]

Beginning writers frequently have trouble in using the demonstrative pronouns *this* and *that* as a means of transition. When *this* or *that* is placed at the beginning of one sentence to refer to something in a previous sentence, ambiguity can result if the pronoun is not followed by a noun. Consider, for example, the following sentence:

Father could get angry, all right, but he had a sense of humor, too. This used to upset Mother, however, for. . . .

It is not clear from reading this sentence whether *this* refers to Father's anger or to his sense of humor. This ambiguity is easily avoided by placing a noun immediately after *this*, specifying to what it refers.

Father could get angry, all right, but he had a sense of humor, too. This sense of humor (or this anger) used to upset Mother, however, for. . . .

Ambiguity does not, however, always result when *this* appears by itself at the beginning of a sentence. So long as the writer's meaning is clear—an important "if"—there is no reason *this* or *that* may not refer to a larger element than a single antecedent, to a clause or even to the general idea of a preceding sentence.

Occasionally, of course, a senator or a congressman becomes involved in a dishonest business affair. This does not mean that politicians are crooks. On the contrary. . . .

EXERCISE 12

A. Underline the transitional expressions in the following paragraphs and indicate in the blanks at the end of each paragraph the relationship that each expression shows.

1. The western is, as most people by this time are willing to acknowledge, a popular myth. And by myth I mean three things. First of all, it is a story whose basic patterns of character, plot, and detail are repeated again and again, and can be so recognized. Secondly, the story embodies and sets forth certain meanings about what is good and bad, right and wrong—meanings regarded as important by those who view and participate in the myth. And thirdly, some of these meanings are veiled by the story, so that one can affirm them without overtly acknowledging them. Some part of the story (or all of it, perhaps) serves to conceal something from the participant—i.e., there is an unacknowledged aspect to the story. There is, therefore, an embarrassing question which never occurs to those in the sway of the myth—the posing of which is precisely the critic's most important task. [From Peter Homans, "Puritanism Revisited: An Analysis of the Contemporary Screen-Image Western," *Studies in Public Communication*, No. 3, University of Chicago, 1961.]

_____

_____

_____

2. Books are as necessary to the student of literature as saw, plane, and hammer are to the carpenter; and just as a carpenter prefers to work and, indeed, does his best work with his own tools, so you will find that you will do your best work with your own tools, your books. Some books, of course, are too expensive for most of us to buy for ourselves and if we want to consult them, we have to go to a library; but money spent on books wisely chosen is money well spent and yields a lasting return. For just as every hammer has its own feel, and the carpenter's favorite hammer has the right feel for him, and just as you know the feel of your own pen or typewriter and experience some sense of strangeness or discomfort when you use another, so you will come to know the feel of your own books and work best with them. [From E. R. Seary and G. M. Story, *The Study of English*, St. Martin's Press, Inc., 1962, p. 83.]

_____

_____

_____

3. The great exception to the routine processes of 19th-century urban expansion was the replanning of the center of Paris. Paris became in fact *the* model 19th-century city. Here, in a consistent organic development that began under Colbert and was carried to a temporary climax under Baron

Haussmann during the Second Empire, a new central structure was created — first in the handsome monumental masonry of the Seine embankment, and then in the great boulevards and new parks. By creating a new outlet for sociability and conversation in the tree-lined promenade and the sidewalk cafe, accessible even to older quarters that were still dismally congested and hygienically deplorable, the planners of Paris democratized and humanized the otherwise sterile Baroque plan. The beauty and order of this new frame, which at once preserved the complexities of the older neighborhoods and opened up new quarters threaded with broad public greens, attracted millions of visitors to Paris and — what was more important — helped increase the daily satisfaction of its inhabitants. [From Lewis Mumford, "The Disappearing City," *The Urban Prospect*, Harcourt Brace Jovanovich, Inc., 1962.]

B. What device or devices does the writer of each of the following paragraphs use to provide coherence? Write your answers in the blanks following each paragraph.

1. A great deal has been said about the duty of the artist to society. It is argued that the poet, the novelist, the painter, the musician, has a duty to the community; he is a citizen like everyone else; he must pull his weight, he must not give himself airs, or ask for special terms, he must pay his taxes honorably, and keep the laws which have been made for the general good. That is the argument and it is a reasonable one. But there is another side; what is the duty of society to the artist? Society certainly has a duty to its members; it has a duty to the engineer who serves it loyally and competently: it must provide him with the necessary tools and must not allow him to starve; it has a duty to the stockbroker who is a competent dealer in stocks; since he is part of a financial system which it has accepted, it must support him and ensure him his due percentage. This is obvious enough. So what is its duty to the artist? If he contributes loyally and competently, ought not society to reward him like any other professional man? [From E. M. Forster, *Two Cheers for Democracy*, Harcourt Brace Jovanovich, Inc., 1951.]

---

2. It is certain, to begin with, that the narrowest trade or professional training does something more for a man than to make a skillful practical tool of him — it makes him also a judge of other men's skill. Whether this trade be pleading at the bar or surgery or plastering or plumbing, it develops a critical sense in him for that sort of occupation. He understands the difference between second-rate and first-rate work in his whole branch of indus-

try; he gets to know a good job in his own line as soon as he sees it; and getting to know this in his own line, he gets a faint sense of what good work may mean anyhow, that may, if circumstances favor, spread into his judgments elsewhere. Sound work, clean work, finished work, feeble work, slack work, sham work—these words express an identical contrast in many different departments of activity. In so far forth, then, even the humblest manual trade may beget in one a certain small degree of power to judge of good work generally. [From William James, *Memories and Studies*, Longman's Inc., 1911. Reprinted by permission of Alexander R. James, Literary Executor.]

_____

_____

3. Major-league baseball is one of the most difficult and precise of all games, but you would never know it unless you went down on the field and got close to it and tried it yourself. For instance, the distance between pitcher and catcher is a matter of twenty paces, but it doesn't seem like enough when you don a catcher's mitt and try to hold a pitcher with the speed of Dizzy Dean or Dazzy Vance. Not even the sponge that catchers wear in the palm of the hand when working with fastball pitchers and the bulky mitt are sufficient to rob the ball of shock and sting that lames your hand unless you know how to ride with the throw and kill some of its speed. The pitcher, standing on his little elevated mound, looms up enormously over you at that short distance, and when he ties himself into a coiled spring preparatory to letting fly, it requires all your self-control not to break and run for safety. And as for the things they can do with a baseball, those major-league pitchers. . . ! One way of finding out is to wander down on the field an hour or so before game-time when there is no pressure on them, pull on the catcher's glove, and try to hold them. [From Roger Kahn, "The Crucial Part Fear Plays in Sports," *Sport* Magazine, August, 1959. Reprinted by permission of Wallace, Aitken, & Sheil, Inc. and *Sport*. Copyright © 1959 by Sport Magazine.]

_____

_____

C. The transitional expressions in the paragraph below have been omitted.

Supply an appropriate word or phrase for each omission.

1. The ability to follow an argument, or to construct one for ourselves, is

what people are usually talking about when they say that the purpose of a

liberal education is to teach you to think. _____ "to

teach you to think" has a silly sound, because, _____

everybody thinks without being taught. We all put two and two together

_____, by some sort of mental chemistry, come out with something new and different, _____ we may be helpless when we try to give an account of the process to ourselves or to explain to someone else the reasons why we should be justified in drawing the conclusions that we believe are sound. _____, we cannot think in the full sense of the word until we can think self-consciously and explicitly —_____, until we can, through argument, lay out the bases, as well as the results, of our thinking and communicate them to other people for their judgment, criticism, and perhaps acceptance. [From Warner A. Wick, "The Argument in Philosophy," *The Journal of General Education*, VII, 1953, p. 82.]

2. Soviet propagandists have long boasted that scientific socialism has created an ideal society in Russia, _____ life in the Soviet Union today, after fifty-six years of communist rule, is hardly utopian. _____, food shortages have periodically plagued the Russians, although more than half the people work the land, as contrasted with about 2 percent in the United States. The Soviet system has, _____ _____, made great strides in transforming a backward, agrarian society into a modern industrial power, _____ it has stifled freedom of thought and expression in the process. Soviet youth, _____, have been given a distorted view of world history and taught to question nothing and to put their faith in communism and the Communist party. Those few who have publicly protested governmental restrictions on artistic expression and free speech have often been denounced and jailed, and sometimes placed in insane asylums. The government has _____ prevented its citizens from reading Western magazines and newspapers. Officials argue that Soviet citizens are not interested in the decadent bourgeois world, _____ these same officials go to great lengths to curb that interest by preventing Soviet citizens from traveling outside Russia. The Soviet system has not created the workers' paradise its propagandists depict, _____ it has made some progress. Political dissidents and artists out of favor are

no longer shot. They are simply put in labor camps or committed to mental hospitals.

D. In the following pairs of sentences the flow of thought between sentences is somewhat obstructed. Rewrite the sentences to make this connection smoother, using the specific devices indicated in the parentheses.

1. Slang is a kind of free-floating language, unrestricted by rules or proscriptions. It is still language. (transition word)

_____

_____

_____

2. In cold, icy weather a small car is very handy. It is seldom trapped by mud or snow, and a slippery grade won't cause it to lose traction. (parallel repetition)

_____

_____

_____

3. A salesperson has to go out and sell and beat the competition. The salesperson must convince customers that the product, the spanking new, chrome-plated, triple-levered Spiro Hydrofax is the best underwater duplicator on the market. (pronoun reference)

_____

_____

_____

4. I'll never forget a bull fight I saw in Mexico City in 1969. By the end of the fight, the horses' insides were spilling out onto the sand of the arena. When the bull fighter killed the bull, the crowd cheered. I was sick to my stomach. (transition word)

_____

_____

_____

5. It is fine for economists and government officials to say that people must lower their expectations. People do not lightly abandon their hopes for a better life. (transition word)

_____

_____

_____

6. The modern American marketplace offers a diversity of goods. We choose cars from an amazing variety of models, makes, and colors; our clothing from many styles, fabrics, and sizes; and the liquor we purchase comes in a multitude of brands, types, and prices. (parallel repetition)

_____

_____

_____

7. Jim Thorpe, an American athlete of Indian descent, excelled in football, baseball, and track at the Carlisle Indian School; won the pentathalon and decathalon at the Olympic Games in Stockholm in 1912; and played professional football and baseball. Thorpe has been regarded by many sports historians as the greatest all-around athlete in American history. (transition word)

_____

_____

_____

8. To utilize the sun and the wind as sources of energy, we must first solve a number of problems. When the sun is hidden by clouds and the wind doesn't blow, there will be no power, so that scientists and engineers must devise a method of storing power from these two sources. (repetition of key term)

_____

_____

_____

9. The Soviet constitution is an admirable code of civil rights. Unfortunately, this code is not being put into practice. (pronoun reference)

_____

_____

_____

10. Terrorist groups that kidnap people for use as pawns to gain political concessions from hostile governments have created difficulties for law enforcement authorities. Protecting innocent lives and preventing further kidnappings presents the police authorities with a dilemma. (repetition of key term)

_____

_____

_____

E. Construct a coherent paragraph using the following notes and any pertinent information you wish to add. Use at least two of the devices for ensuring continuity discussed in this chapter: transitional words, pronoun references, parallelism, and repetition of word and phrase. The notes are not arranged in a logical order in their present listing.

1. massive school integration not easily achieved
2. white resistance serious, black community divided
3. busing a reasonable choice in a small community
4. busing conflicts with concept of neighborhood school
5. added expense of busing a burden to school funds
6. voter resistance to extra taxes needed for busing
7. interferes with participation in after-school activities
8. in large metropolitan areas, busing much more difficult
9. disillusioned blacks believe black control and extra money for ghetto schools a more immediate answer
10. large-scale busing could provoke white flight to distant suburbs

POINT OF VIEW

Point of view defines the position, the point of focus, a writer assumes in relation to the subject. It embraces matters of tone, person, tense, number, and voice. Maintaining a consistent point of view is essential to paragraph coherence. If, for example, you are discussing a subject in the third person, you should stay in the third person unless you have good reason for shifting to first or second person. The same principle applies to tense, number, tone, and voice. A reader is likely to become confused if you change from the past to the present tense, from a singular to a plural noun, from an objective, matter-of-fact tone to a subjective one, or from the active to the passive voice of the verb.

Tone

Tone refers to the attitude a writer takes toward the subject and reader. It can vary widely, depending on his purpose, subject, audience, and interests. A student writing about her roommate might assume an informal, personal, even whimsical tone. If she were discussing the advisability of tax reform, however, her tone would probably be more serious and objective.

The problem of tone is complex, but a knowledge of the distinctive qualities of the formal and the informal tone should be helpful. Formal writing uses a more extensive and exact vocabulary; it frequently alludes to historical and literary events; its sentences are usually longer and more carefully structured than those used in general conversation; and it follows the traditional conventions of English grammar carefully, avoiding contractions, omissions, and abbreviations. Informal writing permits the use of colloquial words and phrases. Its vocabulary is less extensive and its sentences less elaborate, with more of a conversational rhythm. Informal writing also permits the use of first- and second-person personal pronouns (*I, you, we*) and contractions (*I'm, you're, he's*).

The writing demanded of a college student frequently involves the discussion of serious issues and thus requires the more formal, impersonal approach. But whatever tone you adopt, be careful not to shift from an impersonal, serious treatment of your subject to a breezy, colloquial tone, and vice versa, unless there is good reason for doing so and your reader has been adequately prepared for the shift.

INCONSISTENT	CONSISTENT
In the treatment of serious psychological disorders, the therapist seeks to establish rapport with his patient so that he can be induced to take it easy and discuss his problems freely.	In the treatment of serious psychological disorders, the therapist seeks to establish rapport with his patient so that he can be induced to relieve his tensions and discuss his problems freely.
Rocko McNally was a gutty fighter. He could take it as well as dish it out. His capacity for absorbing punishment was, however, exceeded during a match with Kid McGuff. In that contest, he was rendered unconscious in the sixth round by his opponent's right fist.	Rocko McNally was a gutty fighter. He could take it as well as dish it out. His ability to take a punch was, however, exceeded in his match with Kid McGuff, who flattened him with a right in the sixth round.

Person

Pronouns and verbs can be classified according to person, a form whose change indicates whether a person is speaking (first person), is being spoken to (second person), or is being spoken about (third person). A shift in person, as indicated earlier, disrupts continuity. Be careful, therefore, not to change person carelessly from sentence to sentence as you develop your paragraph. Whether you decide to use the informal first or second person (*I, we, you*) or the more formal third person (*he, she, they*), maintain a consistent point of view throughout.

INCONSISTENT	CONSISTENT
To get the most from a lecture, a student should listen carefully and take notes. You should not, however, try to record everything your instructor says. Limit your notes to the important points of the discussion.	To get the most from a lecture, listen carefully and take notes. Don't try to record everything your instructor says, however. Limit your notes to the important points of the discussion.

Tense

A verb undergoes changes in form to show the time of its action or state of being—the past, present, or future. These changes in verb forms are called tenses. Once you have determined the tense you will use in developing your topic, avoid shifting this tense unless you have prepared your reader for the change.

INCONSISTENT	CONSISTENT
After a delay of thirty minutes, the curtain came down, and the orchestra begins to play. Then the house lights dim, and the audience grows quiet.	After a delay of thirty minutes, the curtain came down, and the orchestra began to play. Then the house lights dimmed, and the audience grew quiet.

As noted above, if tense changes occur, the reader must be prepared for them. When he is, they do not violate the principle of consistency. In the following passage the writer maintains a consistent point of view with regard to time even though he changes tense.

The original settlement of Paris *was founded* by a Gallic tribe in the first century B.C. Paris *is* thus about 2000 years old. During these years it *has become* perhaps the most beautiful and cultured city in Europe. In fact, in the opinion of many travelers, it *is* the most beautiful city in the world.

The writer begins in the past tense to establish a point of reference for his remarks. In the second sentence he moves into the present tense to state a fact about Paris at the present time. In the third sentence he shifts to the present perfect tense with *has become,* but this shift does not violate consistency of tense either, for the verb reports a condition—the beauty and sophistication of Paris—that began in the past and continues into the present. And in the last sentence the writer returns to the present tense, again to express a current opinion about his subject.

Number

Number refers to the changes in a word that indicate whether its meaning is singular or plural. As you read over your writing, make certain that you have not shifted number needlessly. If the meaning of a word is singular in one sentence, do not make it plural in subsequent sentences.

INCONSISTENT	CONSISTENT
The student who wants to improve his writing can, in the majority of cases, do so if he puts his mind seriously to it. If they are not willing to make this effort, however, the results will be minimal.	The student who wants to improve his writing can, in the majority of cases, do so if he puts his mind seriously to it. If he is not willing to make this effort, however, the results will be minimal.

Voice

Voice refers to the form of the verb that indicates whether its subject acts or is acted upon. If the subject of the verb acts, the verb is said to be in the *active* voice:

Larry won the election.

If the subject is acted upon, the verb is said to be in the *passive* voice:

The election was won by Larry.

The active voice is used more often than the passive voice, the latter being reserved for occasions when the doer of the action is either unknown or unimportant or when the writer wishes to stress the importance of the receiver of the action. Examine your sentences carefully to make certain that you have used the appropriate voice.

INCONSISTENT

In September of his freshman year, Harvey decided to work thirty hours a week in order to buy a car. After conferring with his counselor about his program, however, the plan was abandoned by him.

CONSISTENT

In September of his freshman year, Harvey decided to work thrity hours a week in order to buy a car. After conferring with his counselor about his program, however, he abandoned the plan.

EXERCISE 13

A. Underline the words and phrases in the following paragraphs that reveal an inconsistency in point of view. In the blanks following the paragraph, identify the error more specifically as one of inconsistency of person, tense, number, or tone; and then correct the error.

1. In a newspaper column in the *Los Angeles Times,* March 2, 1973, Roy Wilkins criticizes the quota system as a means of achieving racial equality for minority groups. Mr. Wilkins argued that it is ridiculous for a member of a minority group to claim that "because they are 40% of the population, they should have 40% of the jobs, 40% of the elected offices, etc." No person of ability, according to Mr. Wilkins, wants his horizon limited by an arbitrary quota or wants to see people promoted or placed in positions for which they are not qualified because of a numerical racial quota. A black-tilted system, Mr. Wilkins adds, does no favor for Negroes. He blasts whitey for discriminating against Negroes over the years, but insists there must not be a lowering of standards. "Guidelines are in order. . . . Persuasion and pressure are in order," he says, but not a quota system that must be crammed down the throats of American citizens.

_____

_____

_____

2. Economists, ecologists, and political leaders have recently been warning the American people not to expect much in the way of an increase in their standard of living in the next few years. Inflation, a slow-growth economy, declining natural resources, and the cost of cleaning up the environment will not permit it. You, wonder, however, whether people accustomed to expect a steady increase in the goodies of life will lightly abandon their hopes for a better life. Judging from the willingness of various pressure groups to exploit society for their own gain, one can assume they won't. Striking policemen in San Francisco, for instance, come in for a lot of flack from the voters because of their pig-headed insistence on a fancy pay raise. They got their raise, nonetheless. Yet one can hardly blame a cop for endangering public safety by leaving the post when a doctor does the same when they feel their interests justify it. And the pushing and shoving goes on in other occupations as well. Sanitation workers, airline mechanics, teachers, firefighters — all jockey to protect their own shares of the American dream, and the devil take the hindmost. Social theoreticians argue that since we live in a world of finite resources, we must decrease our expectations and personal income must be redistributed if we are to maintain the stability of our democratic society. They may well be right, but it is easier said than done.

_____

_____

_____

B. Revise the following sentences to make the point of view consistent.

1. A disturbed individual often thinks that he or she is different from other people. They believe that others don't have feelings of estrangement as they do.

2. Giving a speech is like writing a paper. In writing a paper, you take pains to introduce your subject, develop your ideas about it, and then conclude. When giving a speech, you tell your audience what you're going to tell them, you tell them, and then what you've told them is your conclusion.

3. The accident had been serious. A new Buick had caromed off a stalled truck and, after it had left the road, smashed into a fire hydrant. The driver of the Buick was bleeding profusely from cuts on his face and neck. His left hand had been severed by the front window. Man, what a mess! Finally, I couldn't take it any longer, and I beat it.

4. A famous Englishman once said that the inherent vice of capitalism is the unequal sharing of blessings and that the inherent virtue of socialism was its equal sharing of miseries.

5. Happiness is not something you achieve. It is something that is remembered.

6. Running for political office is a rigorous exercise in self-discipline and dedicated effort. It is physically exhausting, emotionally depleting, and

spiritually demoralizing. If one can't stand the flack of spirited debate, one should forget it.

_____

_____

_____

7. First reread the essay question carefully before you begin to write. Next a few brief notes should be made in the form of an outline of the main points to be covered.

_____

_____

_____

8. The dime novel was a popular literary genre in the nineteenth century. It focused on heroic deeds performed by explorers, trappers, soldiers, and cowboys. It emphasizes excitement and inspiration, especially for the simple-minded.

_____

_____

_____

_____

9. A few years ago when anybody expressed concern over disappearing wildlife, they were often considered sentimental. Fortunately, that is no longer the case.

_____

_____

_____

10. Today when one reads about the early battles for women's rights in this country, you don't laugh.

_____

_____

_____

SUMMARY

Coherence is a third quality of good writing. To make your writing coherent, be sure that your material is organized in some logical order, that your sentences are tied together smoothly, and that your point of view is consistent throughout. The most important quality is the first, for if your thought is developed in an orderly way, you have the basis of a coherent paragraph. Continuity between sentences and point of view are then less of a problem. If your thought lacks logical progression, the addition of transitional expressions and the maintenance of a consistent point of view cannot by themselves supply coherence.

Coherence is the result of careful planning and organization. Therefore, think through what you want to say before you begin to write, and keep your reader in mind as you write. If you build your paragraph as a unit of thought and help your reader to move smoothly from sentence to sentence as you develop that thought, your reader will have no trouble grasping the meaning of your paragraph.

CHAPTER FOUR | Argumentation

The preceding chapters have dealt largely with exposition, the kind of writing that explains. When you wish to convince others of the soundness of your opinions, you will need also the skills of *argumentation.* The characteristics of good exposition — unity, adequate development, coherence — apply as well to argumentation. But persuasive argument requires, in addition, specific knowledge of the processes of logical reasoning and facility in the art of persuasion.

Simply defined, argumentation is a process of reasoning in which a coherent series of facts and judgments is arranged to establish a conclusion. A discussion of argumentation can be complex, for there are many ways of arranging these facts and judgments. However, the discussion that follows will be a simple one, for what is important here is not that you gain a precise knowledge of the variety and complexity of argumentation, but rather that you understand the basic pattern of all arguments and, more important, that you learn to use sound, logical arguments in your own writing.

Any argument, however complex, expresses a relationship between one assertion and another. The first assertion serves as the reason for the second. For example, if you say "Professor Sanderson's exams are difficult. Therefore, I'll have to study hard this weekend," you are making an argument. The second statement is a conclusion based on the first statement.

The first part of an argument may consist of a series of statements:

In the Presidential election of 1964, 62 percent of those Americans eligible to vote actually voted. In the election of 1968, the percentage was 61. And in 1972 it was 55.6. As these statistics reveal, a sizable segment of the American electorate does not take its voting privilege seriously.

In this example, the *conclusion,* the last sentence, follows a series of factual statements. This kind of argument, which proceeds from a study of particulars to the making of a generalization or hypothesis based on those particulars, is called an *inductive argument;* and the supporting particulars that precede the conclusion are called the *evidence.*

The other basic form of argument is called *deduction.* The *deductive argument* has more than one form. A common type, the *categorical syllogism,* begins with a general statement and closes with a particular statement. The supporting reasons in this type of argument are called the *premises.* In the following categorical syllogism the premises provide the basis for the conclusion:

PREMISES   All Americans are freedom-loving.
                George is an American.
CONCLUSION   George is freedom-loving.

A second form of the deductive argument is called the *hypothetical syllogism.* It begins with a conditioned statement which asserts that if a certain condition occurs, something else will follow as a consequence: "If Patricia marries Herbert, she will lose her inheritance." And a third popular type is the *disjunctive syllogism,* which begins with an "either-or" statement: "Either Steve will get a job after high school, or he will go on to college." In the following pages we will discuss in greater detail the nature, uses, and limitations of the inductive and deductive arguments.

THE INDUCTIVE ARGUMENT

As explained above, the inductive argument has two forms: one concluding with a *generalization,* the other with a *hypothesis.* In an inductive argument ending in a generalization, the generalization makes a statement about a class or group of things or people, and the evidence consists of statements about individual members of that class. The inductive argument about American voters on page 121 is of this type. The evidence consists of three statements, each one a particular factual observation about members of the same class, American voters. And the conclusion, ". . . the American electorate does not take its voting privilege seriously," is a more general statement, covering more ground than any of the particular facts that preceded it. This conclusion is an inference about American voters' attitude toward voting; the evidence consists of observations about their behavior at the polls in 1964, 1968, and in 1972.

Here is another example:

EVIDENCE   1. Professor Holliday is witty and perceptive.
             2. Professor Armstrong is witty and perceptive.
             3. Professor Weiss is witty and perceptive.
CONCLUSION   All professors are witty and perceptive.

The conclusion of an inductive argument is a hypothesis when it deals not with a class but with an individual object or situation. In this case the hypothesis attempts to account for the set of facts that preceded it.

EVIDENCE   1. The front lawn of the Hawkins across the street is getting long.
             2. It is getting brown in spots.
             3. Newspapers have been accumulating on the front porch.
             4. The drapes have been pulled across the living room windows.
             5. Today is August 15th.
CONCLUSION   The Hawkins are on vacation.

The conclusion of this argument does not concern a class of things, but rather one particular situation. It is not a generalization, but an inference that attempts to account for the five preceding observations. Each item of the evidence is not a member of a class or group mentioned in the conclusion, as is true of the previous arguments about professors and American voters, but is a description of a different aspect of the appearance of a house on a summer day.

To sum up then, an inductive argument begins with a look at the evidence and ends with a conclusion based on that evidence. It moves from the particular to the general, from fact to conclusion. The distinguishing quality of the inductive argument, however, the characteristic that differentiates it from the deductive argument, is not this movement, but the degree of certainty of the conclusion. The conclusion of an inductive argument *does not necessarily follow* from the evidence. The concluding hypothesis or generalization is only a probability: other conclusions are possible. The conclusion that American voters do not take their voting seriously, because of their failure to turn out in great numbers on three consecutive national elections, may be erroneous. The voters may have been essentially satisfied with the candidates running for election at the time and may not have voted because of general contentment rather than indifference. And another hypothesis is possible to explain the appearance of the Hawkins' house—the family could be away on an emergency visit to a disabled relative.

Evaluating the Evidence of an Inductive Argument

The conclusion of an inductive argument will be sound if there is a logical connection between the evidence and the conclusion. If the connection is missing, the conclusion will not be valid even though it may satisfy the person making the argument. In the following discussion we will examine several general principles that will help you to determine whether the arguments you construct or encounter are sound. We will examine first the argument ending in a generalization.

1. Evidence Supporting a Generalization

The conclusion that any researcher draws from the study of specific cases is necessarily tentative. As you would expect, a generalization based on many samples is more reliable than one based on few. A large sampling, however, does not guarantee a sound generalization. The sampling must be representative as well. For example, to ensure the reliability of his conclusions regarding the popularity of political figures, Dr. Gallup makes certain to poll a sufficient number of voters from a broad cross section of American life. If your own conclusions are to be accurate and persuasive, you must, like Dr. Gallup, support them with an *adequate* and *representative sampling of detail that relates to the subject.*

The generalization on page 123 that all professors are witty and perceptive is clearly not justified by the evidence presented. More than three professors must be observed before a valid generalization about the wit and perceptivity of all professors can be made. A more accurate generalization would result if a more scientific poll of student opinion of professorial wit and perceptivity were conducted. A professional pollster such as Dr. Gallup would have to poll at least several hundred students on campuses throughout the country before reaching a conclusion. But even this kind of poll would not support the original conclusion that *all* professors are witty and perceptive. It might reveal, however, that 34.6 percent, or 41.3 percent, or 61.7 percent, or some other proportion of the group are witty and perceptive.

But the point here is not that you should generalize about a group of people or any group of objects only if you have made a scientific study of the subject. We all live and work by generalizations, and common sense generalizations based on previous experience are ordinarily trustworthy in everyday life. A person who has enjoyed reliable service from automobiles manufactured by one company will likely consider the same make of automobile when he or she is ready to purchase a new one. An investor consistently disappointed by the performance of stock he or she has purchased on the advice of a broker is not likely to continue following that advice. Nonetheless, though scientific precision is not essential in formulating useful generalizations, a generalization based on many samples is obviously more dependable than one based on just a few.

No one can say for certain how much evidence is needed to produce a reliable generalization, but these common sense suggestions should help:

1. Do not generalize too quickly, that is, do not jump to conclusions.
2. Unless your sampling includes all the members of the class you are generalizing about—"All the students in the class scored over 80 on the examination"—or there is widespread agreement about the generalization—"All human beings are mortal"—you should avoid words like *all, every, no one, always* in your generalizations. The generalizations that "Democrats are fiscally irresponsible" or that "Republicans are unconcerned about the welfare of the poor" are simply too sweeping to be persuasive. A more judicious assertion such as "Democrats have often supported a stronger role for the federal government in the regulation of the economy" is more convincing.
3. Study the opinions of experts on a subject when you are uncertain about the adequacy or accuracy of your own data.
4. To measure the soundness of your evidence supporting a generalization, ask yourself whether that generalization has proven a reliable basis for action over a period of time. Students entering college soon discover that success in their studies demands hard work, self-discipline, and perseverance. Such a generalization is clearly dependable. It has been proven true, painfully true, for many generations of students in the past.

The following paragraph is interesting and lively. The evidence is relevant, but there is not enough of it, and what there is, is not sufficiently representative to justify the sweeping generalization in the opening sentence.

You can't trust politicians. Whenever I receive a progress report in the mail from Assemblyman Parker, I wince. During his campaign he lambasted his incumbent opponent for refusing to support legislation restricting campaign contributions. Yet he is now under investigation for diverting money from his campaign funds to redecorate his summer cottage at Blue Lake. It's just as bad at City Hall. Councilman Bertoli has been extolled for years as the pride of our fair city, the symbol of clean, honest, responsible government. But according to yesterday's paper he has been indicted by the Grand Jury for soliciting a bribe from a builder whose proposal to construct a condominium complex at Third and Fairhaven had been rejected by the Council. And then, of course, there's Watergate.

Inexperienced writers who base their conclusions on atypical evidence frequently do so through ignorance of the complexity of their subjects. However, well-informed, experienced writers who select only those facts that support their positions and ignore others that do not are guilty of *stacking the cards*. Writers who stack the cards may cite an impressive body of facts and maintain a fairly objective tone, yet create a false impression of their subjects in the reader's mind because of the facts that they have omitted. Consider, for instance, this appraisal of the strength of communism today:

International communism is a worldwide failure. In Western Europe, Asia, Africa, and Latin America, communism is looking less like the wave of the future and more like the ebbing tide of the past. After the Second World War, Western Europe was ripe for communism — its economy was shattered, its political institutions were weakened, and the Communist party had increased its strength. Yet today Western Europe is a bastion of strength against communist penetration. Its economy, stimulated by the creation of the Common Market agreements, has achieved one of the highest growth rates in the world. And the Communist party, far from dominating the political scene, has steadily declined. Its recent failure to destroy democracy in Portugal is a case in point. Contrast this progress with Soviet failures in agriculture and with the increasing concern and envy of the satellite countries of the industrial strength of Western Europe, and the conclusion is obvious: communism has simply failed in Western Europe.

Nor is the picture much brighter for the Communists in Asia and Africa. Communist China's industrial and agricultural growth has leveled off as a result of its own ineptitude and its disputes with Russia. In Africa both the Russian and the Chinese Communists have tried to spread their brand of revolution in the newly emerging nations, but none has attached itself to the Russian or Chinese orbit. In fact, they are turning gradually to the West for aid and assistance. In South America the efforts of the former Marxist government to transform Chile into a model communist state, an example of what revolutionary socialism can achieve, were also unsuccessful. We in the West, fearful of the communist threat to dominate the world, are too prone to accept the Communists' assessment of their success. For all their boasting that they will bury us, it is likely that they will be the ones to be buried.

Although the writer presents several facts and judgments to bolster his contention that international communism is a conspicuous failure — such as the Communists' inability to penetrate Western Europe, Soviet failures in agriculture, Red China's industrial problems, the unsuccessful attempts of the Communists to subvert the emerging nations of Africa—his presentation is distinctly one-sided. He does not mention, for example, the growth of Soviet influence in Eastern Europe during the past twenty-five years, the increasing prominence of Red China in Asia, the existence of communist Cuba in the Caribbean, the growing strength of the Communist party in Italy, nor the fact that, in spite of the overthrow of the Allende government in Chile, the threat of communist revolution in South America has not been eradicated. A more reliable estimate of the strength of communism would include facts from both sides of the question. In your own attempts at persuasive writing, be sure that you have not omitted important facts that do not support your argument. If you have, revise your paper to present a more balanced view. A balanced view may not be as bold or dramatic as a one-sided view, but it is more effective with informed readers.

The following two paragraphs illustrate a common failing in the writing of persons who feel so strongly about an issue that they fail to provide *accurate, verifiable evidence* to support their generalizations.

Over the past three decades American liberals have been advocating policies and programs that have brought on the ruin of this country. These liberals have continually urged vast federal work projects that obstruct the operation of our free enterprise system, and they have accepted deficit financing as a method of paying for those programs. Deficit financing is never in the public interest, for it produces inflation that destroys the purchasing power of the dollar. Liberals have also sought to hamstring and dictate to American business and industry by urging the creation of regulative agencies such as the SEC, the FCC, and the NLRB. Fortunately, however, Americans are beginning to realize the insidious influence of liberal programs and policies; and with the rebirth of conservatism that is sweeping the country, we will once again achieve our freedom and independence.

This paragraph is a collection of generalizations; it has several topic ideas — government work projects, deficit spending, federal regulative agencies. To revise it satisfactorily, the writer would have to limit herself to one topic and supply the evidence to justify any generalization she makes about it.

The following paragraph also lacks accurate, verifiable evidence:

Americans need not worry about the gloomy predictions of pessimists that disaster awaits us because of population growth and pollution. For example, reports indicate that city air is getting cleaner, not dirtier. One hundred years ago the air over large eastern cities was filled with smoke so thick it could be cut with a knife. Yet today coal smoke has been largely eliminated. Our rivers, lakes, and oceans may not be as pure as they once were, but the amount of water pollution has been grossly exaggerated. Alarmists point to mercury contamination of fish caused by industrial wastes as proof of contamination; yet, as scientists know, the amount of mercury in the oceans today is not significantly higher than it was fifty years ago. Doom sayers predict that world population growth represents a time bomb that will explode and destroy us if population is not curtailed. But according to government reports, the birth rate in the United States has been dropping since 1955. Moreover, demographic experts believe that if the trend is not reversed, the United States will be faced with a serious shortage of people. An objective assessment of these facts invalidates the assumption that pollution and population growth pose a serious threat to the American people.

This paragraph appears to contain a good deal of factual information to support its thesis, but a careful reading reveals that the evidence is tenuous and vague, incapable of justifying the assertion made in the first sentence. Such phrases as "reports indicate," "as scientists know," "according to government reports," and "demographic experts believe" purport to introduce concrete, factual detail. But what specific reports contain information of the quality of city air? What scientists say that mercury contamination of the oceans has not increased? And what demographic experts believe that population growth is not a serious problem? Unless such particulars are supplied, thoughtful readers are justified in withholding their assent to the writer's conclusion.

Evidence that consists of *the opinions or the testimony of others also needs to be carefully examined* to ascertain that opinions are those of a qualified observer — one who is competent in his or her field and able to report observations accurately and objectively. It is a natural human tendency to believe in those who share our opinions and to seek out evidence that confirms these opinions, but it is a tendency that can be fatal to persuasive writing—and to truth. The president of a tobacco company is hardly an unbiased source of information on the health hazards of cigarettes. A chief of police may not be qualified to determine satisfactorily the difference between pornography and literary art. And a retired physicist, however famous for research done in the past, may not be able to speak authoritatively on recent scientific developments.

In the preceding paragraphs we have emphasized the need to supply adequate evidence for generalizations. We have said that the evidence must not be one-sided, that it should be grounded in fact, and that if "experts" are quoted, they must be legitimate authorities. When evidence supporting generalizations meets these tests, a thoughtful reader is likely to consider a writer's arguments carefully.

2. *Evidence Supporting a Hypothesis*

A hypothesis is, as we explained above, a reasoned guess that accounts for a set of facts and that can serve as a basis for further investigation or action. To measure the reliability of a hypothesis, we must examine carefully the facts that the hypothesis is intended to explain, as well as the hypothesis itself. Although a hypothesis may appear irrefutable, one cannot rule out alternative explanations until the favored hypothesis is tested and verified. Consider, for example, the following narrative:

> Joan Addison, the wife of a prominent criminal lawyer, Ben Addison, is found one Sunday morning lying face down on the floor of her living room. She has been shot in the head twice. Her husband discovers the body and reports the crime to the police. Further investigation reveals that Mrs. Addison has been a very successful business woman with extensive holdings in income property. A month before her death, however, she had initiated a suit against a former business partner, Wendall Oliver, charging fraudulent misrepresentation in a business deal. Oliver owns three gambling casinos and in recent years has been associating with big-time gamblers with criminal records. A newspaper article reports that the police believe Mrs. Addison to have been the victim of a professional murderer hired by Oliver.

The speculation that Mrs. Addison has been murdered by an assassin hired by Oliver is the conclusion of an inductive argument, and many readers of the newspaper account of the murder would probably agree with the hypothesis. Yet other hypotheses are possible. The murdered woman's husband may have had her killed, believing her to have committed adultery with Oliver, or Oliver's wife may have hired the murderer for the same reason. If later the fingerprints of an associate of Oliver, a person with a criminal record including violent assault, were found at the scene of the crime, the police hypothesis would be even more convincing. Or if further investigation revealed that Ben Addison had been married before, that his first wife had met a similar fate, and that Addison had recently taken out a new life insurance policy on his second wife, the speculation that Oliver had ordered the murder would be less convincing. In short, a hypothesis is only tentative: it is only as strong as the evidence supporting it. If more than one hypothesis is proposed to explain a set of facts, the hypothesis supported by the most evidence is, clearly, the most persuasive and should be acted upon until proven false. If two hypotheses seem equally plausible, as in the Addison case above, the investigator should maintain an open mind until the evidence favoring one hypothesis preponderates.

Although there are no absolute standards for evaluating hypotheses, for determining precisely when there is sufficient evidence for choosing one hypothesis over another, the following criteria have been suggested by students of inductive argument:

1. The hypothesis should be *internally consistent*, logically possible. The facts should not be contradictory. The conclusion that Oliver had Joan Addison murdered is a logical explanation of her death. All of the circumstances—her suit against Oliver, Oliver's association with known criminals, the way she was killed—do fit together well enough to justify it.
2. If more than one hypothesis is possible, the *frequency of occurrence* of the set of facts the hypothesis seeks to explain must be considered. The hypothesis that has been most frequently set forth to explain similar circumstances in the past is the most probable. For example, when an attractive young man marries a wealthy widow of seventy-five years, one might conclude that he married for love. The conclusion that he married for money, however, is stronger, for such marriages have been prompted more often by greed than by love.
3. The hypothesis should be *capable of verification*. Supernatural causation in human affairs cannot really be tested and is thus an unsatisfactory explanation for human events.
4. When several hypotheses could explain the cause of something, the *simplest* explanation is probably the soundest. A beginning writer whose first novel has been quickly rejected by ten publishers might be correct in concluding that the novel is too in-

tellectually demanding, stylistically original, and honest in its treatment of its subject for editors accustomed to publishing formula fiction for a commercial market. But such an assumption overlooks a simpler explanation — a lack of sufficient creative ability or control in the handling of plot, character, and theme. The latter explanation is simpler and sounder.

A hypothesis that meets these standards is likely to prove useful. Though one should bear in mind that a hypothesis is always tentative, a well-reasoned, logical hypothesis can provide a sound basis for action not only in police work and scientific research but in everyday affairs as well. As Thomas Huxley, a famous British scientist, remarked:

> A person observing the occurrence of certain facts and phenomena asks, naturally enough, what process, what kind of operation known to occur in Nature applied to the particular case, will unravel and explain the mystery? Hence you have the scientific hypothesis; and its value will be proportionate to the care and completeness with which its basis has been tested and verified. It is in these matters as in the commonest affairs of practical life; the guess of the fool will be folly, while the guess of the wise man will contain wisdom.*

Common Inductive Fallacies

A *fallacy* is an error in reasoning. It refers to an argument that violates a principle of logical inference. In the following discussion we will examine briefly a few common types of faulty induction.

A writer who makes a *hasty* or *sweeping generalization* fails to supply enough evidence to support his generalization. The writer of the paragraph on politicians (p. 125) is guilty of this error. The solution to this problem is not to avoid generalizations for fear they might be exaggerated, but to make certain your generalizations are justified by the supporting evidence. Reread your papers carefully, therefore, and revise any extravagant unsupported statements.

UNSUPPORTED

Segregation of the races has been a part of Southern life for decades. Therefore integration will not work. You can't change human nature.

---

* "The Method of Scientific Investigation," from *Darwiniana* by Thomas Henry Huxley (London: D. Appleton and Co., 1896).

IMPROVED

Segregation of the races has been a part of Southern life for decades. Successful integration will therefore take time. Southern attitudes and behavior patterns must be changed, and such changes are not made quickly.

Generalizations drawn from *statistical data* need to be examined carefully because statistics can be manipulated to yield a variety of interpretations. For example, if a man increases his contribution to a charitable organization from five dollars to ten dollars a year, he can legitimately claim to have increased his contribution 100 percent, an impressive figure to one not aware of the actual amount involved. Or suppose that a report of the income of individuals working in a small business firm indicates that the average annual salary of the employees is $10,000. This information by itself might lead you to the conclusion that these employees were well paid and that the owners of the firm were justified in refusing to consider salary increases. Upon closer examination, however, you discover that, of the ten persons working in the firm, five earn $5,000 annually, three $6,000, one $7,000, and one $50,000. The average annual salary of this group is in fact $10,000, but for most people *average* connotes *typical;* yet only one of the ten persons actually earns $10,000 or more in a year. The typical salary in this case would be closer to $6,000 than $10,000. Be careful, then, when you use statistics to establish or reinforce a generalization. If one figure of a set of figures is considerably larger or smaller than the others (for example, the $50,000 salary in the case cited above), taking an average of them will distort their relationship. In such cases it would be more informative to report the *median* value (the middle figure in an odd number of figures) or the *mode* value (the figure that appears most frequently). In short, use statistics as honestly and informatively as you can, lest your reader suspect that you have manipulated them to suit your purpose.

Thus far we have discussed the hasty generalization and the generalization based on deceptive statistics. A third type of faulty induction is the *post hoc fallacy,* which occurs when we assert that one event caused another because it preceded it. If one thing occurs before another, it does not *necessarily* cause the latter. This kind of inference is known technically as the *post hoc, ergo propter hoc* fallacy ("after this, therefore because of this"), or, more simply, the *post hoc* fallacy. That one political administration was in office when war broke out, for example, does not mean that that administration brought on the war. The fact that the number of capital crimes committed in a state decreased the year after capital punishment was abolished does not prove that the change in punishment caused this decrease.

It frequently happens, of course, that one event *is* the cause of another. When a person collapses after being struck a blow on the head, it is fairly clear that the first event, the blow, caused the second, the collapse. But establishing a causal relation between two events is often more difficult. It is especially difficult in the field of economics. Here is an example:

> The recent tax cut passed by Congress was obviously warranted. The American economy was given the shot in the arm it needed. Retail sales and business profits have gone up, the rate of unemployment has gone down, and our foreign trade has expanded.

To prove that the tax cut specifically caused the improvement in retail sales, business profits, and foreign trade would necessitate the examination of a considerable body of facts. An economist, or an experienced reader, would want to know, for example, the effect of seasonal variation in consumer spending, government spending, the business community's confidence in the economy, and the actions of foreign governments in reducing tariffs, before he could accept such an explanation.

One of the methods of paragraph development presented in Chapter Two was the *analogy,* a comparison of two things that are unlike but that have similar attributes. Analogy is frequently used as evidence to support an argument.

> Recently *The New York Times* reported an address by Supreme Court Justice Powell in which he deplored the deterioration of the nation's moral fiber and cited, as an example, the open selling of student themes and term papers to college and university undergraduates.
>
> It seemed to me a rather feeble for instance, and one which a politician (and let's not pretend the Supreme Court isn't a political as well as a judicial body) might well eschew. If it's all right for the President of the United States to hire people to write his speeches on which the fate of nations may rest, why isn't it equally acceptable for a college student to hire someone to write his term papers, on which nobody's fate rests but his own? [From Ed Zern, "Exit Laughing," *Field and Stream,* December, 1972, p. 160.]

This example illustrates an important fact about analogies: they frequently break down by ignoring basic differences in the two things compared. This analogy between the selling of term papers to college students and the President's hiring of speech writers, as an illustration, overlooks an important difference between these two practices. The awesome responsibilities and complex, time-consuming duties that burden a President of the United States make it impossible for him to write every speech he gives and, therefore, justify the employment of speech writers. The public understands and accepts the practice. A college student is not so burdened. Moreover, the obvious fraudulence of falsifying the authorship of term papers and the prohibition against it are clearly understood and accepted by most college students. When you use analogy to buttress an argument, therefore, keep its limitations in mind. It can clarify a point made in an argument, but it cannot settle the argument.

EXERCISE 14

A. Factual information and the testimony of experts could be used to support the following statements. In the blanks below each statement list the kinds of factual information you could use and an authority you might consult.

EXAMPLE   Nurses are underpaid.

1. statistics on nurses' income — average salary and general range of income, from beginning to veteran nurses' income
2. comparison of nurses' income with that of other professional persons — doctors, lawyers, and so forth
3. opinions of leaders of American Medical Association; American Nurses Association; Secretary of Health, Education, and Welfare

1. Medical schools screen their applicants very rigorously.

_____

_____

_____

2. Young men are the most reckless drivers on the road.

_____

_____

_____

3. The increase in the price of crude oil over the past four years has had a harmful effect on American domestic and foreign policy.

_____

_____

_____

4. Top-flight professional basketball players are well-paid.

_____

_____

_____

5. The mass media of communication — newspapers, magazines, radio, television — exploit the violence and sordidness of American life for commercial gain.

_____

_____

_____

6. Physics 23A is a difficult course at this college.

_____

_____

_____

7. Tennis has become an increasingly popular sport in the United States these past ten years.

_____

_____

_____

8. Investing in the cattle business is a risky business.

_____

_____

_____

9. Americans have yet to come to grips with the energy crisis.

_____

_____

_____

10. Law enforcement is a hazardous occupation in the United States.

_____

_____

_____

B. Classify the following arguments as inductive or deductive.

1. Leslie Ordway telephoned his wife on a Friday evening to tell her he had to make a quick trip to Mexico City on business for the bank. This news surprised his wife, for the bank had never sent him on a business trip before. Moreover, she didn't know he had a passport. The following Monday morning an audit uncovered the fact that Ordway's trust accounts were $115,000 short. In his comments to the press the bank manager charged Ordway with embezzlement. _____

2. Ian MacTavish is a thrifty, hard-working man. But that is not surprising. He was born in Scotland, as were all his ancestors. _____

3. San Francisco is one of my favorite vacation spots. My husband says it's because I love trolleys. _____

4. In 1973 Janet Harris got a job as an interior decorator's assistant to supplement the family income. In 1974 her picture appeared in the local paper in connection with a competition she had won in interior decorating. In 1975 the firm she worked for increased her salary by $750 per month.

Janet Harris is obviously doing well as an interior decorator. ___*Deduct*___.

5. Harvey Potts drives a late model sports car to college, spends his summers in Europe, and always has plenty of pocket money to spend. His parents

must be well-to-do. _____

C. Classify the following inductions as hypotheses or generalizations.

1. In the past seven months Dan Jenkins, an investigative reporter for an Eastern newspaper, has been talking to farmers in the South. In a recent newspaper column he concluded that Southern farmers will not support a

liberal for President in the up-coming election. _____

2. The automobile, a 1951 Dodge coupe, was found at the side of a lonely desert road just outside of Indio, California. Its hood was up, its windows pitted. Sheriff deputies discovered the body of an elderly man, the owner of the automobile, lying face down in the sand, an empty canteen by his side, three miles from the main road. He had apparently been caught in a sandstorm when his car stalled, then started off across the desert,

ran out of water, and died of dehydration. _____

3. I'm not driving to Boulder again. Every time I do something goes wrong

with my car. _____

4. The tennis team at State University is really smashing. These past three months I've been visiting a buddy at State, and we've watched some

matches each time I've been to see him. _____

5. Americans are certainly more permissive today than they were twenty-five years ago. The number of pornographic movie houses has increased, as well as the number of "adult" bookstores selling dirty books. Moreover, unmarried mothers are far more common today, the divorce rate is up, and

convicted criminals have been getting lighter sentences. _____

D. Weaknesses in inductive arguments discussed in the preceding pages include the following:

1. sampling of evidence too selective
2. lack of sufficient evidence
3. incompetent or biased authority
4. generalization based on deceptive statistics
5. hasty, sweeping generalization
6. *post hoc* fallacy
7. false analogy

137

Identify the weaknesses in each of the following arguments by placing one or more of the numbers in this list after it.

1. Of the 213 letters written in response to the editor's request for a show of support for the college ski team, 98 percent favored increasing the athletic budget for the sport. It is clear from the sampling of student opinion revealed in this response that skiing is a very popular sport and deserves greater budgetary support from the administration. _____

2. Sex education courses are the work of the devil and should be eliminated. They stimulate and excite youthful passions that should be subdued. In a recent survey over 10 percent of the high school students subjected to the course in their senior year had illegitimate children within the next five years. _____

3. All I said was that the voter registration drive was nothing but another pressure group run by a bunch of frustrated, discontented party bosses, and this jerk slugs me. Just goes to show you, Harry, you can't really talk seriously to politicians. They're too emotional. _____

4. Of course I use Haut Monde After-shave Cologne. I read in a magazine advertisement the other day that Jim Winkle, the professional basketball star of the Port Royal Rockets uses it, and he's a very savvy guy. _____

5. The Pure Food and Drug Act has prevented the sale of food and drugs harmful to the body. Congress should also investigate ways to eliminate unscrupulous publishers. _____

6. Seven students took an examination, and their scores were 98, 65, 62, 61, 59, 58, and 50. The average score was thus 64. Thus only two of the seven students taking this examination scored above the average. Obviously most of these students hadn't studied very hard for the examination. _____

7. The cause of the increase in malpractice suits against doctors is simply that the medical profession has been too lax in weeding out the incompetent members of the profession. _____

8. I've been working in the Complaints and Adjustment Department of Stacy's Department Store for fifteen years, and I have learned that women shoppers are surly and ill-tempered. _____

9. Who says playing college football builds character? My two roommates are on the team, and they are the sloppiest, laziest rowdies I know. _____

10. Heretofore I have placed little faith in the stories of bureaucratic mismanagement in Washington, but lately my eyes have been opened. My friend's uncle has a

brother working in the Department of the Interior (fish and game section) who claims that the examples of in-efficiency and stupidity he has heard about would cause a businessman to explode in anger. Obviously we need a new administration in Washington.   _____

E. Provide at least two hypotheses to explain the set of circumstances narrated below. What additional facts would make one of them more creditable?

Monty Sayers, basketball coach of Western State University, has had two very successful seasons in his first two years as coach. His star guards, Mike Warren and Larry Harper, were selected as the two best guards in their league. Be-cause of his coaching success, he urged the student athletic council to ap-prove an emergency request for funds so that he could attend a coaching seminar at Northeastern University. The council approved his request, though the vice-president of the council, Sydney Walton, objected. That spring Sayers attended the seminar at Northeastern, his alma mater, where he was an All-American basketball player. On returning to Western, Sayers informed the athletic director and the president of the college that he would be leaving Western to become head basketball coach at Northeastern University in the fall. In his sports column in the college paper, the sports page editor revealed that Warren and Harper had applied for admission to Northeastern University four weeks before Sayers had appeared before the student athletic council.

F. Read the following selections carefully and evaluate the logic used in each. In the space provided after each passage identify the main weak-nesses in the arguments advanced. In particular, look for examples of in-sufficient evidence, false analogy, and a biased source of evidence.

1. In recent months doctors have been complaining about the rising cost of malpractice insurance. This clamor from physicians, however, is a smoke-screen to hide medical incompetence and a ploy to increase doctors' fees. The American public pays doctors handsomely, and deserves competent treat-ment. Doctors lay much of the blame for the increased costs on lawyers, who, they say, often receive exorbitant fees when they win a judgment for their clients. Yet I've talked to three friends of mine who are trial lawyers, and they say that idea is nonsense. According to them, the problem is simply the failure of the medical profession to weed out incompetents, and I agree. For all the money they make doctors ought to be able to assure their patients of expert care. With all the modern equipment at their disposal doctors shouldn't make mistakes. If this country can put someone on the moon, our doctors should be able to cure human ailments.

_____

_____

_____

2. Before my son went away to college last fall, I had a serious talk with him about the importance of studying hard so that he could get into medical school. I was therefore a little worried by his last letter, for he told me that he wanted to join a fraternity next year. I was afraid fraternity life would interfere with his studies and that he might give up his plans to become a doctor. I decided to talk to some of the fellows at the office whose sons had gone to college. Talbot told me that his son had joined a fraternity in his junior year and that it had not affected his studies adversely. On the contrary, joining a fraternity had been good for him: it had taken some of the rough edges off the boy, taught him some manners, and given him some polish. Wortham was similarly enthusiastic. His son had been out of college three years, but the contacts he had made in the fraternity had helped him tremendously in his business career. Like myself, Wortham had been worried about wild fraternity parties and crazy stunts when his son expressed the desire to join a fraternity; but his boy assured him that fraternity life was not like that at all. After thinking it over carefully, I have come to the conclusion that fraternity life is good for young men going to college.

---

3. Conservation groups are planning to battle with power companies over a tract of land in Wyoming, North Dakota, and Montana that may hold as much as 200 billion tons of coal. What worries environmentalists, as well as ranchers and farmers in the area, is that in the process of strip mining the coal the power companies will despoil and scar the land. Spokesmen for the utility companies, however, discount such fears. They have promised to restore any land that needs it. Moreover, this country needs the coal to produce energy, and the utility companies have paid for the right to mine the coal. To deny them the right to the coal would be to deny citizens the right to use their own property as they see fit. This right is fundamental to the American way of life. The evidence clearly supports the power companies. They should be allowed to strip mine the coal.

G. Write a short paper, one or two paragraphs, on one of the following topics, using an inductive process. That is, investigate the subject firsthand, recording your observations in note form, consult relevant experts, and then write up the results of your investigation. Present your data first and your conclusion near or at the end of your paper.

1. student attitude toward ecology as revealed in the appearance of the campus

2. student participation in intramural sports, social clubs and organizations, political clubs, community service groups
3. student use of library facilities
4. public transportation in your community
5. quality and availability of living accommodations for students on and off campus
6. part-time work done by students

H. The following excerpt from *The Adventures of Sherlock Holmes* by Sir Arthur Conan Doyle reveals Holmes's ability to make unerring hypotheses to account for the details he observes. Dr. Watson, Holmes's friend and fellow adventurer, narrates.

I did not gain very much, however, by my inspection. Our visitor bore every mark of being an average commonplace British tradesman, obese, pompous, and slow. He wore rather baggy grey shepherds' check trousers, a not over-clean black frock-coat, unbuttoned in the front, and a drab waistcoat with a heavy brassy Albert chain, and a square pierced bit of metal dangling down as an ornament. A frayed top-hat, and a faded brown overcoat with a wrinkled velvet collar lay upon a chair beside him. Altogether, look as I would, there was nothing remarkable about the man save his blazing red head, and the expression of extreme chagrin and discontent upon his features.

Sherlock Holmes' quick eye took in my occupation and he shook his head with a smile as he noticed my questioning glances. "Beyond the obvious facts that he has at some time done manual labour, that he takes snuff, that he is a Freemason, that he has been in China, and that he has done a considerable amount of writing lately, I can deduce nothing else."

Mr. Jabez Wilson started up in his chair, with his forefinger upon the paper, but his eyes upon my companion.

"How, in the name of good fortune, did you know all that, Mr. Holmes?" he asked. "How did you know, for example, that I did manual labour? It's as true as gospel, and I began as a ship's carpenter."

"Your hands, my dear sir. Your right hand is quite a size larger than your left. You have worked with it, and the muscles are more developed."

"Well, the snuff, then, and the Freemasonry?"

"I won't insult your intelligence by telling you how I read that, especially as, rather against the strict rules of your order, you use an arc-and-compass breastpin."

"Oh, of course, I forgot that. But the writing?"

"What else can be indicated by that right cuff so very shiny for five inches, and the left one with the smooth patch near the elbow where you rest it upon the desk."

"Well, but China?"

"The fish which you have tattooed immediately above your right wrist could only have been done in China. I have made a small study of tattoo marks, and have even contributed to the literature of the subject. That trick of staining the fishes' scales of a delicate pink is quite peculiar to China. When, in addition, I see a Chinese coin hanging from your watch-chain, the matter becomes even more simple." [From "The Red-Headed League," *The Adventures of Sherlock Holmes*, The Heritage Press, New York, 1950, pp. 266–267.]

Using this excerpt as a model, construct a brief scene in which a character of your invention, a brilliant detective, forms one or more hypotheses to explain a number of details he observes.

THE DEDUCTIVE ARGUMENT

In the preceding pages we have studied the relation between inductive reasoning and writing, but, as we mentioned there, writing uses both induction and deduction. In induction you examine a number of particulars and formulate a conclusion to account for them. If the conclusion is a generalization, you can then, by means of a deductive process, apply the generalization to a particular case. For example, if you learn through personal experience that salespeople are extroverts, you can apply this information to the salesperson sitting beside you on a train and anticipate a lively conversation. Your reasoning process could be patterned as follows:

1. Salespeople are extroverts.
   The person sitting opposite me is a salesperson.
   Therefore, the person sitting opposite me is an extrovert.

This argument is an example of the *categorical syllogism* described earlier. It has three parts: two premises followed by a conclusion. The *major premise* makes a general statement about something — an object, an idea, a circumstance. In the example above "Salespeople are extroverts" is the major premise. The *minor premise* contains further information about one of the terms in the major premise. "The person sitting opposite me is a salesperson" is the minor premise of the example. And the *conclusion* is a logical inference to be derived from the premises. The last sentence in our syllogism is its conclusion.

The movement of this kind of syllogism is from the general to the specific, from a statement about a larger group to a statement about an individual member of that group. The categorical syllogism simply classifies an individual, object, or idea as a member of a group and assumes that the object so classified will have qualities of that group. Unlike the inductive argument ending in a generalization, which moves from the specific to the general, the categorical syllogism moves from the general to the specific. But the essential difference between a deductive and an inductive argument is not this direction of movement but the fact that the conclusion of a deductive argument can be proven to follow necessarily from the premises, whereas, as explained earlier, the conclusion of an inductive argument is always somewhat uncertain.

Here are two examples of a syllogism, with their premises and conclusions indicated.

2. MAJOR PREMISE   All human beings are mortal.
   MINOR PREMISE   Socrates is a human being.
   CONCLUSION   Socrates is mortal.

3. MAJOR PREMISE   All Communists believe in the eventuality of war between socialist and capitalist states.
   MINOR PREMISE   Hensley Cartright is a Communist.
   CONCLUSION   Hensley Cartright believes in the eventuality of war between socialist and capitalist states.

The major premise commonly precedes the minor premise, but it need not. In the following syllogism, for example, the minor premise appears first:

4. MINOR PREMISE   Tippy is a cocker spaniel.
   MAJOR PREMISE   Cocker spaniels are dogs.
   CONCLUSION   Tippy is a dog.

If the conclusion of a syllogism is a logical extension of the ideas contained in the premises, as it is in each of the four syllogisms presented above, the conclusion is said to be *valid*. But a valid conclusion is not necessarily a *true* conclusion. Consider, for example, the following syllogism:

5. MAJOR PREMISE   All Irishmen have fiery tempers.
   MINOR PREMISE   Timothy Carmody is an Irishman.
   CONCLUSION   Timothy Carmody has a fiery temper.

The conclusion in this syllogism is valid: it follows necessarily from the premises, but the major premise is inaccurate—all Irishmen do not have fiery tempers—and thus the conclusion is untrue. A syllogism can yield a true conclusion only when both the premises are true and the conclusion is valid. In the following discussion we shall consider the characteristics of the valid conclusion and the true conclusion in greater detail.

The Valid Conclusion

The first rule of a valid syllogism is that it must have only three terms, each of which appears twice in the three statements. A *term* is the subject or predicate of a statement. In the syllogism

6. MAJOR PREMISE   All children are curious.
   MINOR PREMISE   Stephen is a child.
   CONCLUSION   Stephen is curious.

the two terms in the major premise are *children* and *curious,* and the term *child,* which appears in both the major and minor premises (but not in the conclusion), is called the *middle term.*

Another rule of a valid syllogism is that the middle term must be "distributed" in one of the premises; that is, the middle term must appear in a premise that includes or excludes all the members of a class. The term *chemists,* for example, is distributed in each of these statements:

All chemists are intelligent. No chemists are intelligent.

In syllogism 6 above, the term *children* is distributed in the first premise, "All children are curious." In the following syllogism the middle term, *honorable men,* which appears in both major and minor premises, is distributed in the second premise:

7. MAJOR PREMISE   All honorable men are open-minded.
   MINOR PREMISE   All writers are honorable men.
   CONCLUSION   All writers are open-minded.

But consider this next syllogism:

8. MAJOR PREMISE   All Italians are music lovers.
   MINOR PREMISE   Gilbert is a music lover.
   CONCLUSION   Gilbert is an Italian.

The middle term in this syllogism, *music lover,* is not distributed in either premise. Neither premise includes or excludes all those who love music. The term *Italian* is distributed in the major premise, but it is not the middle term. Therefore, the conclusion does not follow, and the syllogism is invalid. A conclusion that does not follow from the premises of a deductive argument is called a *non sequitur.*

A syllogism in which the meaning of the middle term changes from major to minor premise also produces an invalid conclusion. In the following argument the meaning of *democratic* differs in the two premises, and the conclusion is thus a *non sequitur.*

9. MAJOR PREMISE   All political leaders having democratic sym-
                    pathies are popular.
   MINOR PREMISE   Governor Fagin has Democratic sympathies.
   CONCLUSION   Governor Fagin is popular.

The pattern of valid and invalid deductions is usually clarified by the use of diagrams. For example, in syllogism 6 the major premise states "All children are curious." If we draw a small circle to represent children and a larger one to represent individuals who are curious and then place the small circle within the larger, we can diagram the relationship between children and curiosity contained in the major premise.

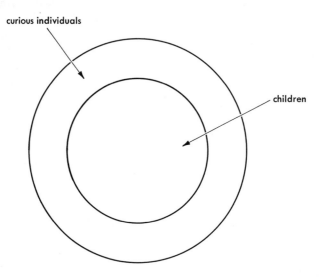

By drawing a still smaller circle to represent Stephen and placing it within the circle marked "children," we can diagram the minor premise, "Stephen is a child."

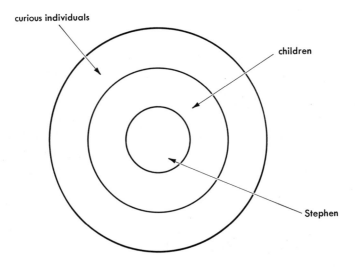

As the diagram now shows, the smallest circle is necessarily included in the largest circle, and the conclusion is thus valid: Stephen *is* curious.

Using the same system of circles to diagram syllogism 8, we can clearly see that its conclusion does not follow. The major premise, "All Italians are music lovers," can be represented thus:

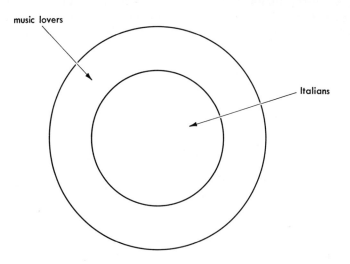

The minor premise, "Gilbert is a music lover," allows us to place the circle representing Gilbert any place within the larger circle: it does not have to be placed within the circle marked "Italians."

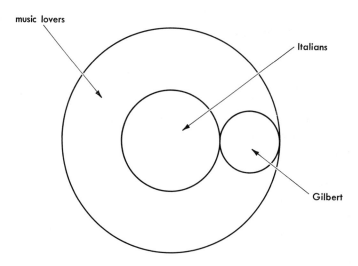

Therefore, the conclusion "Gilbert is an Italian" is a *non sequitur*—it does not follow.

The True Conclusion

We said earlier that a valid conclusion is not necessarily a true conclusion. The premises must also be true before the argument can
produce a true conclusion, and true conclusions are essential to convince a careful reader. The more firmly rooted in accurate, verifiable
observation the major premise is—the more thorough the process of
induction that produced it—the sounder it is. "All human beings are
mortal" is an accurate premise; it is a generalization born of universal
human experience. Any syllogism based on it may yield a true conclusion. Few premises, however, are so unquestionably accurate.
Arguments based on such premises as "The United Nations is a plot
to subvert the United States," "Blondes have more fun," and "Americans are crass materialists" are likely to result in faulty conclusions.
In constructing deductive arguments, therefore, make certain that
your premises are accurate and your reasoning valid. In other words,
make certain that your syllogisms yield true conclusions. A logically
deduced conclusion derived from unsound premises is like a well-
constructed house built on a poor foundation. Both are likely to
collapse.

The criteria for the valid conclusion and the true conclusion mentioned above do not cover all syllogisms, but they are sufficient for
our purposes here. Several common problems related to the deductive argument, however, should be considered. These include the
concealed premise and the fallacies of begging the question, over-
simplification, and evading the issue.

The Concealed Premise

A writer or speaker frequently omits one of the premises of a
syllogism. Such a syllogism is not necessarily unreliable, but it
presents a problem for an inexperienced writer or listener, who may
accept an argument without realizing it is an argument and that its
implied premises must be tested. The statement "Realtors make
good school-board members; therefore, Henry Babbit should be
elected to the school board" is a syllogism with its minor premise,
"Henry Babbit is a realtor," missing. In such cases the minor premise is easily supplied and tested. Greater care, however, needs to be
taken when the major premise is missing. The statement "The current tax bill before Congress should be passed: the United States
Chamber of Commerce favors it" contains the concealed premise that
the kind of tax legislation promoted by this organization is good for
all Americans and should be enacted. The truth of this assumption is
open to serious question—many economists would certainly oppose

it—and because it is so central to the argument, the writer cannot ignore it without weakening his case.

Examine your own arguments, then, to see that they are not based on hidden, untenable premises. And when reading or discussing an issue with others, analyze the arguments proposed for the same purpose. If any contain concealed premises, supply the missing premises and test them for accuracy.

Begging the Question

An argument that begs the question assumes as proved the point the argument ought to be establishing. This fallacy is also known as the circular argument, for the conclusion of the argument is merely a restatement in the same words or synonyms of the basic premises, leaving readers no wiser at the end of the argument than they were at the beginning. The following arguments illustrate this fallacy:

1. Literature courses are useless because they are a waste of time.
2. Senator Barker is corrupt and should be removed from office because the United States Senate is no place for a dishonest man.
3. Atheists are really hopeless because people who don't believe in God cannot be very bright.

Frequently this kind of argument requires several sentences to complete it.

Self-reliant citizens do not need federal aid to help them pay for their children's education or their medical bills. People with independence of spirit and initiative can provide these things by themselves. Therefore they do not need federal aid for education or medical bills.

To the careless or uninformed reader this passage may appear to constitute an effective argument against federal aid for education and medical care, when in fact it contains no argument at all. The last sentence, meant to be a conclusion, simply reasserts the idea contained in the two preceding sentences. As this example illustrates, the lack of logic and supporting evidence makes the circular argument a poor risk with careful readers.

Oversimplification

Oversimplification is a common fallacy in argumentation. Persons who are frustrated with the complexity of modern life and who desire simple, direct solutions for its problems commonly indulge in over-simplification. The rabid segregationist who regards civil rights legislation as indicative of the federal government's desire to tyrannize the South, the radical reactionary who believes that abolishing the income tax would solve the unemployment problem, and the military leader who feels that American security can be ensured by simply brandishing nuclear weapons — all these views are oversimplifications of complex problems.

A characteristic tendency of people who oversimplify is to divide people, ideas, and things into two or three sharply contrasting groups. There is a right way and a wrong way to do things, a moral way and an immoral way. Democrats are good, Republicans are bad; the federal government is bad, local government is good; economic systems are socialistic or capitalistic. The weakness of such conclusions is that they omit the possibility of other alternatives: they reject any middle ground between these polar positions. Few economic systems in the world, for example, are either purely capitalistic or purely socialistic. When revising your papers, therefore, reexamine your statements to see that you have not oversimplified issues. An intelligent reader will not be persuaded by simple answers to difficult questions.

Evading the Issue

The evidence used to prove an argument not only must be sufficient and representative, as explained earlier; it must be pertinent as well. When a writer or speaker engaged in a dispute presents evidence that does not relate to the point of his opponent's argument, he commits the error of evading the issue. An arguer who evades the issue often uses one of the following techniques: (1) the "smear" technique, (2) the "transfer" technique, and (3) the "bandwagon" technique. In the first of these, the arguer attacks the man instead of dealing with the issues he introduces. The following arguments illustrate this technique:

1. I'm against Senator Ryun's amendment to the Constitution. He's simply a fascist reactionary who would like to see the country run by big businessmen.
2. You can disregard Bill Olson's warning on automation; he's a typical labor boss trying to stop economic progress.
3. I'll never understand what movie critics see in Leslie Windgate. She's irritable, conceited, and immoral. She's been married five times.

In each of these examples, the writer uses abuse rather than rele-

vant evidence to support his argument. Leslie Windgate's unsuccessful married life and her unpleasant disposition, for example, are
not relevant considerations in an evaluation of her acting ability.

The transfer technique involves an appeal to authority—to a famous
name or universally sanctioned idea—to validate an argument. Advertisers, newspaper editors, and politicians frequently attempt to gain
acceptance for a product or a point of view by using this technique.

1. Linebacker Bull McCrunch smokes Crisp cigarettes. He reports . . .
2. Movie actress Ariel Tempest washes her hair regularly with
   Bubble shampoo.
3. Elvis Presley, discussing recent developments in modern art,
   said . . .
4. Benjamin Franklin would never have approved of such a huge
   federal debt.

All these statements illustrate the fallacy of the simple appeal to
authority. What Benjamin Franklin said may no longer be relevant in
today's world. Nor can one accept Elvis Presley's opinion on art simply because he is widely known. Of course, if these individuals were
quoted on subjects within their competence, this fallacy would not
apply. Linebacker McCrunch's knowledge might be relevant to a discussion of football and Elvis Presley's to one about contemporary
popular music.

Speakers or writers who ignore the issue through an appeal to the
passions and prejudices of the crowd use the bandwagon approach.
For example, a political campaigner frequently modifies his approach
to accommodate his audience. In Harlem he appeals to his listeners
as blacks; in Arkansas he appeals to them as farmers. The following
passage illustrates this emotional appeal:

> I know that the people of this great nation will not reject a man
> who has throughout his entire public life worked and fought for
> the good of America. I know that they will not reject a man of
> the people, a man dedicated to the preservation of American free-
> doms against the threat of godless communism.

Advertisers also use this device:

> Don't be left behind. Join the crowd and switch to Blitz beer.

The weakness of the bandwagon approach is that in its appeal to
the emotions of the audience it submits little or no factual or logical
evidence for consideration.

The Loaded Question

The fallacy of the loaded question, like that of begging the question, assumes the truth of something that has not been proved, but it also implies wrongdoing on the part of the person to whom the question is directed. One can't answer such a question without incriminating himself or committing himself to something he doesn't believe. The question "Why does the government permit big unions to seriously disrupt the economy of this country?" assumes two things, that big unions do seriously disrupt the economy of the country and that the federal government permits it, both of which have not been established. One really cannot reply to such a question. The best he can do is to point out that the question is faulty because it contains unproven assumptions.

EXERCISE 15

A. Place a V after each of the following syllogisms that has a valid conclusion and an I after each one that has an invalid conclusion. (Diagram each syllogism on a piece of scratch paper to help you determine its validity.) Indicate the cause of an invalid argument by writing one of the following numbers next to an I: (1) undistributed middle term, (2) more than three terms used, (3) shift in meaning of middle term.

EXAMPLE All dogs drool.
Hugo drools.
Hugo is a dog.   <u> I, 1 </u>

1. All dogs have fleas.
Rover is a dog.
Rover has fleas.   <u>   </u>

2. All tigers have tails.
My cat has a tail.
My cat is a tiger.   <u>   </u>

3. All laws that promote inflation are bad.
This law promotes inflation.
This law is bad.   <u>   </u>

4. All patriots love their country.
Dorothy loves her country.
Dorothy is a patriot.   <u>   </u>

5. Most rich people are content.
Cynthia is rich.
Cynthia is content.   <u>   </u>

6. Some novelists are good psychologists.
All scholars seek the truth.
All novelists seek the truth.   <u>   </u>

7. Candidates with democratic sentiments will make good Congressmen.
Dennis Cardwell is a Democrat.
Dennis Cardwell will make a good Congressman.   <u>   </u>

8. All smoking nuisances should be eliminated in this city.
Erich is a smoking nuisance in this city.
Erich should be eliminated.   <u>   </u>

9. All men of distinction drink Old Tennis Shoes.
Herbert Parkenfarker is a man of distinction.
Herbert Parkenfarker drinks Old Tennis Shoes.   <u>   </u>

10. All rats like cheese.
Roberta likes cheese.
Roberta is a rat.   <u>   </u>

B. In the following syllogisms some conclusions are true, some are valid, and some are invalid. If the conclusion is true, place a T in the blank after it. If it is valid, place a V in the blank, and if it is invalid, place an I in the blank. (Remember that a true conclusion and a valid conclusion follow logically from the premises, but only a true conclusion follows from sound, accurate premises.)

1. All movie stars are wealthy.
   Debbie Torch is a movie star.
   Debbie Torch is wealthy. ___T, V___

2. Successful persons are those who have contributed to the welfare of their fellow men.
   Dr. Salk has contributed to the welfare of his fellow men.
   Dr. Salk is a successful person. ___I, T___

3. All persons who misreport their income on their income tax forms are unethical.
   Some Americans misreport their income on their income tax forms.
   Some Americans are unethical. ___V, T___

4. All students who cheat on their examinations are dishonest.
   Frank is dishonest.
   Frank cheats on his examinations. _____

5. All human beings are fallible.
   English instructors are human beings.
   English instructors are fallible. _____

6. People who obey laws they don't like deserve praise.
   Jim Ratlin, a trucker, doesn't like the 55 mph speed limit, but he obeys it.
   Jim Ratlin deserves praise. _____

7. All extroverts are conceited boobs.
   Peter Per Scott is a conceited boob.
   Peter Per Scott is an extrovert. _____

8. All sorority girls are sophisticated and well-bred.
   Marilyn is a sorority girl.
   Marilyn is sophisticated and well-bred. _____

9. All superstitious people are ignorant.
   Barbara is wise.
   Barbara is not superstitious. _____

10. All students who can use their native language effectively are apt to succeed in college.
    John Cassady can use his native language effectively.
    John Cassady is apt to succeed in college. _____

$$A = B$$
$$C = A$$
$$C = B$$ V

$$A - B$$
$$C = B$$
$$C = A$$ INV

C. The following items are deductive arguments with hidden major premises. Supply the missing premise of each argument.

EXAMPLE   Of course Clampson Dental Cream is good; it's advertised in *Peek* magazine.

Missing Premise Products advertised in *Peek* magazine are good.

1. Andre Bouton is quite a lover, but then he is a Frenchman.

Missing Premise _____

2. Professor Walker is obviously an excellent teacher. Her students rave about her sense of humor.

Missing Premise _____

3. Of course he favors wage and price controls. He's an intelligent man.

Missing Premise _____

4. *The Bountiful Boudoir* is obviously a good book; it sold more than 2 million copies the first year of its publication.

Missing Premise _____

5. Buy Volkswagen. It never dates you.

Missing Premise _____

D. The following statements are deductive arguments with missing minor premises. Supply the missing premise in each argument.

1. Eloquent senators make fine presidents. Therefore, Senator Connors should be elected president.

Missing Premise _____

2. Circus performers lead exciting lives. Lorraine's life must be very exciting.

Missing Premise _____

3. A liberal arts course is a waste of time. Consequently, I'm not going to major in history.

   Missing Premise _____

   _____

4. Football players need to be big and beefy. Therefore, Kerrigan ought not to go out for football.

   Missing Premise _____

   _____

5. People who smoke Puritan cigars have discriminating taste. Larry obviously has discriminating taste.

   Missing Premise _____

   _____

E. Identify the fallacies in the following arguments.

1. This measure, ladies and gentlemen, which will permit the Department of Agriculture to sell surplus American wheat to the Russians, is nonsensical, if not treasonable. The American people are not going to approve of helping to feed their sworn enemies, the Communists. On the contrary, patriotic Americans will protest this measure as an exercise in stupidity.

   _____

2. Good grief, Genevieve, why do you always insist on having your own way?

   _____

3. Love it or leave it, Harry. That's what I say. If these young punks don't like what's going on in the country, they ought to get out. Who needs 'em?

   _____

4. Wayne is shy and introverted because he's afraid to assert himself.

   _____

5. National League baseball players agree. Sheffield razor blades make shaving a sheer delight.

   _____

USING REASONS TO DEVELOP A PARAGRAPH

The information on inductive and deductive reasoning just presented should help you use reasons to develop a paragraph. The persuasiveness of this type of paragraph depends on the soundness of the reasoning that supports the central idea. Make certain, therefore, that your inductions are based on a sufficient number of relevant facts, examples, and judgments. If you quote authorities, make certain they are competent and objective. Be careful, too, that your deductions follow logically from sound premises.

Read the following paragraphs carefully, and note how the writer of each uses reasons to develop and clarify his central idea.

First Reason

Second Reason

Third Reason

The new creed, with its dismissal of free discussion and its conviction that violence will mystically generate policy and program, represents an assault on rationality in politics — an assault based on the ultimate proposition that rights and wrongs in public affairs are so absolute and so easily ascertainable that opposition can be legitimately destroyed. This assault on the Bill of Rights and on libertarian democracy is in my judgment wrong, because no one is infallible. It is stupid, because the beneficiaries of this view will not be the idealists of the left but the brutalists of the right. It is dangerous, because it represents a reversion to and rationalization of the strain of hatred and violence in our own national tradition: the politics of lynch law against the politics of Lincoln. It is a vote for the worst against the best in our political ethos. [From Arthur Schlesinger, Jr., "America 1968: The Politics of Violence," *Harper's Magazine*, August, 1968, p. 23.]

First Reason

Second Reason

Third Reason

The phrase "conquest of nature" is certainly one of the most objectionable and misleading expressions of Western languages. It reflects the illusion that all natural forces can be entirely controlled, and it expresses the criminal conceit that nature is to be considered primarily as a source of raw materials and energy for human purposes. This view of man's relationship to nature is philosophically untenable and destructive. A relationship to the earth based only on its use for economic enrichment is bound to result not only in its degradation but also in the devaluation of human life. This is a perversion which, if not soon corrected, will become a fatal disease of technological societies. [From René Dubos, *A God Within*, p. 40. Charles Scribner's Sons 1972.]

EXERCISE 16

A. The following subjects are often the bases of sharp differences of opinion. Select one of the subjects and develop a paragraph in which you argue one side of the question. In your topic sentence make clear the position you favor.

1. liberalizing abortion laws
2. liberal versus occupational education
3. working wives
4. working while attending college
5. granting citizenship to illegal aliens who have lived ten years or longer in the United States
6. athletic scholarships for college students
7. installment buying
8. capital punishment
9. tougher sentences for juvenile law-breakers
10. forced busing to achieve racial integration

B. Francis Williams is the manager of a bank in a small city in the Southwest. He is a hard-working, energetic man, well-liked and respected by his staff because of his genuine interest in their progress and his even-handed treatment of them. He demands good work, and he is fair and honest in his criticism and praise of his subordinates. In the community he has a reputation for enlightened civic responsibility. He is the chairman of a committee seeking ways to improve job opportunities for members of minority groups. The committee is composed of four persons, himself and three members of minority groups. An opening for a management trainee occurs in the bank, and he has narrowed the list of applicants to two persons: one, the son of one of his employees, Helmut Schmidt, the other, the daughter of a close friend who is a member of the committee mentioned earlier. The young man, a college graduate, has an impressive educational background and excellent references, but no experience in banking. The young woman is enrolled as a part-time student at a local community college where she is studying business administration. Her present employer, as well as her former employers, speak well of her initiative, conscientiousness, and seriousness of purpose. Whom should Mr. Williams hire?

Write a paragraph indicating the course of action you think Mr. Williams should take. Think carefully about the consequences of the course you propose, as well as those you reject, and develop those thoughts into specific reasons to support your choice.

PERSUASION

Persuasive writing is not solely a matter of logic: it is also a matter of language and attitude. To convince your readers, you must attend to the clarity, honesty, and emotional impact of your arguments as well as to their logical construction. Much persuasive writing deviates from the truth to appeal to the prejudices of an audience, but writers who continually engage in emotive, slanted writing ultimately damage whatever cause they serve. This does not mean, of course, that you should never use emotional words in your writing. On the contrary, effective persuasion sanctions—even demands—an emotional plea at times. Moreover, strict objectivity is impossible—no one can completely avoid the influence of his subjective preferences. Nonetheless, your basic purpose in argumentative writing is to elicit from your reader a favorable response to your ideas, and you are not likely to obtain such a response from thoughtful readers if they think your emotions have blurred your objective regard for the truth.

Definition of Terms

The most important element in persuasive writing is clarity, for regardless of how logical your arguments may be or how responsibly you have dealt with the facts, if you have not expressed yourself clearly, you will not convince many readers. Accurate, precise definition of terms is especially important. Be careful, therefore, to define clearly those terms central to your meaning. In particular, such words as *liberty, freedom, truth, justice, liberal, conservative, radical* and *propaganda* need to be pinned down, for they are subject to a wide range of interpretation. The following illustrates this problem:

> The American people have been deceived about the nature of their government. They have been taught that the United States is a democracy, when actually it is a republic. Consequently, proposals to modify the system of electing a president to make it more democratic are irrelevant.

This passage is vague because of the writer's failure to tell us what he means by *democracy* and *republic*. Since both terms can be used to describe forms of government in which the power resides in the voters who elect representatives to decide public issues, the writer should specify the sense in which he is using these terms if he is to convince rather than confuse us. The revision below eliminates this confusion, although one may still not agree with the conclusion.

A republic is commonly defined as a form of government in which the voters elect representatives to meet and decide public issues. A pure democracy is a form of government in which the voters themselves assemble in one place to decide these issues. Accepting this distinction, we can describe the United States as a republic rather than a democracy. Hence, proposals to modify the system of electing a president to make it *more* democratic are irrelevant.

VAGUE

It is time Americans recognized the danger of extremist groups. These subversives should be controlled before they do real damage to the American way of life.

IMPROVED

Political groups and organizations that advocate radical measures to meet the problems of our time threaten the stability of American life. What constitutes a "radical" measure is, of course, open to dispute, but most Americans would probably agree that the term could be applied to such actions as bombing federal buildings to express opposition to governmental policies; eliminating welfare programs, Medicare, and the Social Security system; and establishing local guerrilla "armies." Although radical groups have a right to express their opinions and gain adherents to their cause, they should be watched carefully to see that they do not break any laws.

Exaggeration

Exaggeration is a fairly common element in much argumentative writing. Editorial writers, political figures, salesmen, and advertisers use exaggeration to stimulate interest in their ideas or products. The use of the superlative is such a common feature of motion picture advertising, for instance, that the public is almost reluctant to attend a film that has not been described in advance publicity as "stupendous," "breathtaking," "the picture of the decade." Political columnists sometimes indulge in exaggeration to emphasize their opinions, as the following passages illustrate:

Willkie was never a real Republican. . . . He was a socialist Democrat, the tool of Democratic subversives who tried to convince Americans that Soviet Russia was a real ally. He is largely to blame for the United Nations. He was used by Roosevelt to further . . .

Congressman Barnes is one of the loudest of the TVA zealots. He comes from Tennessee, where the TVA is a lush local racket. . . .

Such phrases as "the tool of Democratic subversives," "to blame for the United Nations," "loudest of the TVA zealots," and "lush local racket" tell us much more about the writer's state of mind than about his subject. Here are examples of exaggerated statements with suggested revisions:

EXAGGERATED	REVISED
The foreign aid program succeeds in doing nothing but pouring money down a rat hole. It is a vast giveaway program that aids no one.	Our foreign aid program needs to be examined carefully to see if we cannot eliminate some of the waste and mismanagement in its operation.
The lessons of history are unmistakable. Either we reduce our tax rate, or the United States faces imminent economic chaos and disaster.	Reducing tax rates in the countries of Western Europe after the Second World War provided a needed stimulus to their economies. In all likelihood, lower taxes in the United States would produce a similar expansion.

Emotive Language

A problem related to clarity involves loaded or slanted words, words that reveal the user's feelings and attitudes, his approval or disapproval. Loaded words are rather commonly used in situations in which people's feelings are aroused—political discussions, for example. In the opinion of one person, Senator Jones is intelligent, firm, compassionate in his regard for the underdog. To another he is opinionated, rigid, a maudlin do-gooder. In the course of a conversation between these two persons, people working in Washington, D.C., might be referred to as intellectuals or eggheads, public servants or bureaucrats, faithful employees or time-servers.

The following passage provides further illustration of the use of loaded words. The opinions are those of a Mississippi circuit judge on the subject of Mississippi whiskey.

If when you say whiskey you mean the devil's brew, the poison scourge, the bloody monster, that defiles innocence, dethrones reason, destroys the home, creates misery and poverty, yea, literally takes the bread from the mouths of little children; if you mean the evil drink that topples the Christian man and woman from the pinnacle of righteous, gracious living into the bottomless pit of degradation and despair, and shame, and helplessness, and hopelessness, then certainly I am against it.

But if when you say whiskey you mean the oil of conversation, the philosophic wine, the ale that puts a song in their hearts and laughter on their lips, and the warm glow of contentment in their eyes; if you mean Christmas cheer; if you mean the stimulating drink that puts the spring into the old gentleman's step on a frosty, crispy morning; if you mean the drink which enables a man to magnify his joy, and his happiness, and to forget, if only for a little while, life's great tragedies, and heartaches, and sorrows; if you mean that drink, the sale of which pours into our treasuries untold millions of dollars, which are used to provide tender care for our little crippled children, our blind, our deaf, our dumb, our pitiful aged and infirm; to build highways and hospitals and schools, then certainly I am for it.

This is my stand, I will not retreat from it. I will not compromise. [From Kenneth Vinson, "Prohibition's Last Stand," *The New Republic*, October 16, 1965, p. 11.]

As these differences of opinion about Senator Jones and about whiskey reveal, special feelings and associations attach to words. The person who approves of Senator Jones describes him in words that arouse favorable feelings — *intelligent, fair, compassionate*. The person who disapproves of the senator uses words that arouse unfavorable feelings — *opinionated, rigid, do-gooder*. Similarly, one who refers to whiskey as the *oil of conversation*, the *philosophic wine*, *Christmas cheer* clearly approves of it; one who regards it as the *devil's brew*, the *poison scourge*, the *bloody monster* rather clearly disapproves of it. The suggestions and associations that cluster about a word make up its *connotative* meaning. The connotations of *firm*, for instance, are positive: the word suggests determination, courage, solidity — all attractive qualities. The connotations of *rigid*, however, are negative: it suggests stubbornness, inflexibility, a narrow-minded unwillingness to compromise — all unattractive qualities. The tendency to use words with favorable connotations, honorific words, in referring to what we like can be seen in a common practice today, the substitution of a word with more pleasant associations for one that conveys a less pleasant reality. These sugar-coated words and phrases are called *euphemisms.*

Words have *denotative* meanings as well as connotative meanings. The denotative meaning of a word signifies its literal, explicit meaning—the object or idea it stands for. The denotation of "firm" and "rigid" is the same—unyielding, difficult to move. The distinction, then, between the connotative and denotative meaning of a word is that its connotation includes the feelings and attitudes associated with it; its denotation does not. And, as illustrated, the connotation of a word may be positive or negative.

Emotive words, words with strong connotations, vary in their power to arouse feeling. *Political nonconformist, reactionary, fascist*—all evoke feelings of anger in many people's minds. But *fascist* evokes a stronger reaction than does *political nonconformist.* Because emotive words can powerfully influence people's opinions, some writers employ them frequently to condemn persons and ideas they do not like. By using loaded words such as *traitor, subversive, demagogue,* and the like, they hope to lead their readers into forming unfavorable opinions of their subjects without examining the supporting evidence. As a method of neutralizing the appeal of loaded language, Max Black, a well-known authority on critical thinking, suggests that the reader identify the emotive terms of a passage and then replace the original emotive words with neutral terms (words with little or no emotional charge) or with terms that have contrasting connotations.* As an illustration, the emotive words in the following passage are listed in the first column, and the corresponding neutral words and words with contrasting connotations are listed in the next two columns.

It is time for decent Americans to speak out against an absurd tax system that permits greedy, conniving oil tycoons and assorted "fat cats" to escape paying their fair share of income tax. Legislators, tax lawyers, and other frauds who defend the practice spew the garbage that tax loopholes provide an essential stimulus for the monied class to invest in business and industry to keep the economy healthy. Hogwash and soul butter! Congressmen who utter such drivel selfishly want to protect their sources of campaign contributions; tax lawyers don't want to lose their fat fees for finding such deductions. Until the mass of taxpayers vigorously protest this outrage, they will continue to be the patsies in this annual income tax con game.

* Max Black, *Critical Thinking*, 2nd ed., Prentice-Hall, Inc., 1952, pp. 172–76.

EMOTIVE WORDS	WORDS WITH MORE NEUTRAL CONNOTATIONS	WORDS WITH CONTRASTING CONNOTATIONS
decent	ordinary	conventional
absurd	incongruous	unique
greedy	money-conscious	thrifty
conniving	manipulating	shrewd
fat cats	rich businessmen	wealthy investors
frauds	deceptive individuals	clever individuals
spew the garbage	say	argue with conviction
loopholes	deductions	tax incentives
monied class	persons with money	the financially independent
hogwash and soul butter	not so	I sincerely disagree
drivel	opinions	convictions
selfishly	simply	understandably
fat	large	handsome
outrage	injustice	established custom
patsies	victims	sufferers
con game	collection process	assessment

Substituting more neutral words for the emotive words of the original produces this version:

It is time for ordinary Americans to speak out against an incongruous tax system that permits money-conscious, manipulating oil tycoons and assorted rich businessmen to escape paying their fair share of income tax. Legislators, tax lawyers, and other deceptive individuals who defend the practice say that tax deductions provide an essential stimulus for persons with money to invest in business and industry to keep the economy healthy. Not so! Congressmen who utter such opinions simply want to protect their sources of campaign contributions; tax lawyers don't want to lose their large fees for finding such deductions. Until the mass of taxpayers vigorously protest this injustice, they will continue to be the victims in this annual income tax collection process.

This version communicates the essential meaning of the first version, but its emotional overtones have been dampened so that the reader is less likely to be bulldozed by the implications and innuendos of the original. A second revision, this time using the "purr" words of the third column in place of the "snarl" words of the first, yields the following:

It is time for conventional Americans to speak out against a unique tax system that permits thrifty, shrewd oil tycoons and assorted wealthy investors to escape paying their fair share of income tax. Legislators, tax lawyers, and other clever individuals who defend the practice argue with conviction that tax incentives provide an essential stimulus for the financially independent to invest in business and industry to keep the economy healthy. I sincerely disagree! Congressmen who utter such convictions, understandably, want to protect their sources of campaign contributions; tax lawyers don't want to lose their handsome fees for finding such deductions. Until the mass of taxpayers vigorously protest this established custom, they will continue to be the sufferers in this annual income tax assessment.

The point of this discussion, it should be stressed, is not that emotive language should be avoided because it is customarily used by those who distort and exaggerate. On the contrary, persuasive writing deliberately and legitimately appeals to the emotions of the reader. Many respected writers and speakers employ emotion successfully to persuade others of the truth of their ideas. But it must be used with care. If your readers believe that you are substituting emotion for credible evidence, that you are trying to browbeat them into agreement, they are apt to dismiss your arguments as biased and unreliable. In short, deal honestly with your readers. If you use an emotional appeal, let them see the evidence that justifies it.

EXERCISE 17

A. Read the following passage carefully. Underline the emotive terms, list them in the blanks at the end of the passage, and then supply words with opposite, or nearly opposite, connotations in the second list.

Standard off-the-rack liberals drip tears of compassion for the wife of a convicted murderer facing execution in the gas chamber, but few of these salon socialists put on such a display for the wife of a murdered policeman. The monster who coldbloodedly slays the owner of a liquor store or brutally molests a child invariably evokes sympathy as his case moves through the courts. The victims of these moral outrages are forgotten. Sentimental sociologists and cocktail-hour psychologists spout the nonsense that capital punishment represents "cruel and unusual" punishment and should therefore be ruled unconstitutional. What about the "cruel and unusual" punishment suffered by those criminally assaulted? Do-gooders and other mental midgets maintain the fiction that life imprisonment is a more effective and moral deterrent than capital punishment. The truth is, however, that few killers spend the rest of their lives in prison, a fact conveniently overlooked by those who agonize over violence. The degenerates who murder decent citizens deserve no such concern. They should be brought to justice and executed.

<table>
<tr><td align="center">EMOTIVE WORDS</td><td align="center">WORDS WITH CONTRASTING
CONNOTATIONS</td></tr>
<tr><td>_____</td><td>_____</td></tr>
<tr><td>_____</td><td>_____</td></tr>
<tr><td>_____</td><td>_____</td></tr>
<tr><td>_____</td><td>_____</td></tr>
<tr><td>_____</td><td>_____</td></tr>
<tr><td>_____</td><td>_____</td></tr>
<tr><td>_____</td><td>_____</td></tr>
<tr><td>_____</td><td>_____</td></tr>
<tr><td>_____</td><td>_____</td></tr>
</table>

B. The following appraisal of the threat of international communism is one-sided, for it omits important facts about communist failures. The appraisal presented on p. 126 is also one-sided. Using facts appearing in each of these slanted versions, write a balanced view of the danger of the communist threat.

International communism seriously threatens the survival of Western civilization today. Since the end of the Second World War, it has dramatically extended its influence throughout the world. In Poland, Czechoslovakia, Bulgaria, Rumania, and Hungary the Communist Party dominates the lives of the people. It has also gained considerable strength in Italy, and though it has not yet succeeded in overturning the moderate political parties in Portugal, it remains a threat to democratic government there. In Asia the most populous nation on earth, China, is now communist and exerts a baleful influence on India, Thailand, Vietnam, and Cambodia along its borders. Nor has the Western Hemisphere remained unpolluted. Cuba has become a communist beachhead in the Caribbean, aiding and fomenting revolutions in Central and South America against democratically elected governments. Constitutional government in Brazil and Argentina is also threatened by communist agitation, and if Brazil and Argentina fall, South America cannot be saved. And the military suppression of the Marxist government in Chile has not hurt the communist cause. A realistic evaluation of the growing power of worldwide communism yields an unavoidable conclusion: unless the West can muster its strength immediately to dam the communist flood, its civilization will be washed away like that of Rome.

C. Opposite each of the words or phrases in the following list, place a word or phrase with roughly the same denotation as the word in the left-hand column but with a different connotation as directed.

  EXAMPLE   tax loophole (more favorable) — tax incentive

1. an elderly spinster (less favorable) _____

2. flexible (less favorable) _____

3. taxpayers' money (more favorable) _____

4. law officer (less favorable) _____

5. soldier of fortune (less favorable) _____

6. crammed hard but flunked the text (more favorable) _____

   _____

7. devout (less favorable) _____

8. maid (more favorable) _____

9. made a pile of dough on slick real estage deals (more favorable)

   _____

   _____

10. garbage dump (more favorable) _____

D. The words in the following lists have about the same denotation, but their connotations vary markedly. Rank them in order of the favorability of their connotations, beginning with the word with the most favorable associations.

1. stupid, ignorant, innocent, naive, uninformed

_____

2. obese, fat, portly, stout, pudgy

_____

3. playboy, swinger, bon-vivant, hedonist, lecher

_____

4. eccentric, odd, non-conformist, weird, individualistic

_____

5. devout, godly, sanctimonious, religious, pious

_____

E. The following list contains ten euphemisms (sugar-coated words or phrases substituted for words and phrases with less favorable connotations). For each euphemism select the word or phrase for which it is a substitute.

1. refuse station _____

2. anti-social act _____

3. word processer _____

4. substandard housing _____

5. career apparel _____

6. petrochemical dispenser _____

7. daughter of joy _____

8. language facilitator _____

9. affected by an inordinate use of intoxicants _____

10. passed on _____

F. Read the following two selections carefully, one an advertisement and the other an editorial, and write a short paper on either one evaluating its persuasiveness. Keep these questions in mind as you write your paper: Does the writer support his judgments with factual or illustrative detail? Is he fair with the opposition? Does his argument rely on emotion rather than reason? Support your judgments with specific illustrations.

We Mass-Produce Almost Everything in This Country — Except Character

It used to be that when you wanted something, you worked to earn it. Now you stage a riot to get it given to you at someone else's expense.

If your father or grandfather lost his job, he took whatever work he could get, and he went (probably walked miles) to where there *was* work — *any* honest work — being done. Now hordes of relief "clients" refuse a job unless it is to their liking, and they demand the job be brought to them in their community.

This nation was built by immigrants (beginning in the 1600's and earlier) who struggled here for opportunity, and would have scorned the false idea of "something for nothing." Now it seems to be an almost universal (and all too often the only) ambition.

It used to take a lifetime of gruelling work and scrimping for a family or a country to earn a little surplus, a taste of security. Now mobs of stupid "students" and whole "emerging nations" demand they be given, out of *your* earnings and with no effort on their part.

"Minority groups" all over the earth seem to think the world owes them everything they want. So vicious destructiveness makes necessary higher taxes to pay for more police to protect decent citizens; higher taxes for playgrounds and parks, which hoodlums promptly make unsafe; higher taxes for schooling for gangs who don't seem to want or are unable to be educated. The minority groups whose rights no one seems to consider are the taxpayers and decent citizens — who may have been pampering evil too long. [From an advertisement for the Warner & Swasey Company. *Newsweek*, September 6, 1965, p. 1.]

President Ford tried to get a responsible tax-spending bill from Congress but in the end he was out-maneuvered again by double-talking Democratic leaders.

This has been the story of President Ford since he took office. His good intentions are seldom translated into action. When the skirmish ends, the President almost always winds up holding a bagful of weasel words from Congress, but no constructive action on spending.

This time Mr. Ford gave up on his demand that Congress make "spending cuts equal to any tax cuts . . ."

The resulting bill is such an undisguised sham that it boggles the mind to imagine how the Democrats had the nerve to put it in writing. It is even more baffling how Republican leaders in both houses agreed to this verbal claptrap and how President Ford happily accepted this totally hedged nonpledge. [From the St. Louis *Globe Democrat*, December, 1975.]

G. The following newspaper column comments upon the British and French governments' efforts to obtain landing rights in the United States for the Anglo-French supersonic transport, the Concorde. Read the column carefully, and in a paragraph or two comment upon the soundness of the writer's reasoning. Are his arguments clear, supported with factual detail, relevant? Does he rely on emotion rather than reason to make his point?

Does he present both sides of the question? Does his conclusion follow logically from the data he presents? Support your judgments with specific reference.

Washington — The Concorde, the Anglo-French supersonic transport, was begun 13 years ago as a hands-across-the-channel gesture of, well, concord between ancient rivals.

As a political tactic it was banal and barren. As an economic program it has become a $2.5 billion fiasco.

And now the Concorde is straining relations between the United States and two nations that could ill-afford to build it and now cannot sell it. The question is: Should we let them use it here?

They have built 10 Concordes, which cost more than $50 million each. Six more are in production. Demand is not brisk: The only sales have been to the state-owned British and French airlines.

Concorde fares are 20 percent higher than current first-class fares, in part because it carries only 108 passengers, and because it consumes two to three times as much fuel per seat-mile as do subsonic aircraft. But it will halve the current seven-hour flying time from New York to London.

It will attract businessmen and others for whom a little bit of time is worth a lot of money. But it is only feasible on routes with a lot of such traffic. The crucial route is over the North Atlantic.

But the Concorde is noisy, arguably too noisy for flights into New York's Kennedy and Washington's Dulles airports. Yet if we ban the Concorde from them, we will be effectively banning it from the essential route. This probably will make the Concorde so unprofitable that its government sponsors may be forced to cut losses by killing the plane.

The Concorde makes no sonic boom within 200 miles of takeoff and landing. So as regards Kennedy and Dulles it would be a noisy subsonic aircraft. How noisy is unclear.

A London report charges that on takeoff the Concorde is six times as loud as the new wide-body jets, and three times as loud as Boing 707s. Concorde supporters say these noise levels are produced by pilots who have not mastered noise-abatement techniques.

According to current plans, the Concorde would not be noisy often in the United States. British Airways and Air France are seeking a total of two flights a day to Kennedy and one to Dulles. Of course, if the Concorde is as profitable as its backers say it will be, they will clamor for more flights to these and other airports — Miami and Dallas, for example.

The Concorde represents the triumph of politics over common sense in Britian and France. It is the sort of silliness that only governments can manage, and it is valuable primarily as a monument to the truth of this maxim: Prudent people are sensibly skeptical of so-called commercial projects that cannot be produced by private markets.

And the Concorde is still a preventable mischief: We could cripple and probably kill it. But doing so would seem to be, and probably would be, unfair.

There can be little doubt that if the U.S. government had not suffered a

171

moment of lucidity, during which it killed the American SST, our noise restrictions would have been tailored to permit our SSTs to operate. Furthermore, it is obvious that a significant portion of the Concorde's high-spending passengers will be skimmed away from U.S. carriers—TWA and Pan Am—which can ill-afford to lose them. So banning the Concorde would be viewed by Britain and France as protectionism carried out under the cloak of environmentalism.

The United States has produced 80% of the jet aircraft in commercial use in the world today. We who have benefited so much from nondiscriminatory attitudes regarding our products cannot gracefully destroy the profitability of other people's products.

True, we might be doing a favor to British and French taxpayers if we banned the Concorde. But the U.S. government, the wastrel of the Western world, has neither a duty nor a right to correct the misdirection of foreigners' resources. [From a column by George F. Will, "It's a Noisy Mistake—Theirs, Not Ours—. But Let's Not Rub It In." © *The Washington Post*. Reprinted by permission.]

SUMMARY

Effective argumentative writing requires the ability to think logically—to reason correctly from the evidence or premises—and to persuade others to accept your reasoning. In this chapter we have briefly investigated the basic processes of reasoning, induction and deduction, and examined some common fallacies in reasoning. We have said that generalizations resulting from induction must be adequately supported; that is, there must be sufficient, relevant evidence to justify the generalization, and the evidence must be representative, accurate, and verifiable. And if testimony is used, the authority quoted must be qualified and objective. Hypotheses that are logically possible, in accord with normal human experience, verifiable, and not overly complicated are likely to provide sound bases for action or further investigation. Deduction produces true—and therefore useful—conclusions when the premises are accurate and the conclusions valid. To persuade your readers to accept your arguments, you must convince them of your integrity, and the best way to accomplish this is to express yourself clearly and honestly. Choose your words carefully, therefore, and avoid highly charged language.

CHAPTER FIVE | The Theme

In your college work you will frequently be asked to write compositions of several hundred words. Research papers, expository essays, book reviews, final examinations — all require more extensive development of an idea than is possible in a single paragraph. The problems you will encounter with the longer paper are not radically different from those of the paragraph. An essay of 500 words demands the same careful attention to unity, development, and coherence as does the paragraph. But, because of the greater length and complexity of such a composition, you will find it necessary to plan it more thoroughly. To make your meaning clear to a reader, you will have to think more carefully about what you want to say and how you want to say it.

Many students who have trouble with writing assignments seem to think that writing is an inherited talent, that those who write well simply have a facility for it and that if one lacks this facility, there is little to be done about it. However, good writing does not simply result from natural ability: it results from thoughtful planning, intelligently directed effort, and writing and rewriting. Those who write well, as most professional writers would testify, do not reach for a piece of paper and begin to write lucid, polished prose. On the contrary, they must plan and revise their work carefully. In short, good writing requires not genius, but a willingness to learn and a steady application of what has been learned.

There are no simple, mechanical rules to follow in writing a theme; a system that works well for one writer may not work well for another. But by following a series of steps, you should be able to avoid many of the frustrations and false starts that plague students who begin to write with no plan of procedure. These steps include:

1. selecting a topic
2. narrowing the topic
3. thinking through the topic
4. gathering and organizing material
5. outlining
6. writing the first draft
7. revising the first draft
8. preparing the final copy

As you develop skill in writing themes, you will be able to modify and condense these steps into three or four operations, especially for themes written in class; but until you develop such proficiency, you would be wise to follow each step carefully. We will consider these steps in order.

1. SELECTING A TOPIC

Sometimes you will be allowed to select your own topic; at other times a topic will be assigned. When it is assigned, be certain you know precisely what is required before you begin. Knowing what the subject or question calls for is especially important when you are writing an essay examination or a theme in class, for time limitations do not permit extensive revision if you have misunderstood the subject. For example, if the assignment calls for a discussion of the causes of the French Revolution, concentrate on the causes of the revolution. Do not devote a major portion of your paper to a description of the cruelties perpetrated upon the aristocracy during the Reign of Terror.

When you can select your own subject, choose one from your own experience or one that arouses your interest. Like many students, you may underrate the value of your experiences, but a personal experience that taught you something about life frequently makes an interesting theme topic. It need not be an earth-shaking event, one that illuminated a profound idea, but simply an experience that had meaning for you and that you would like to share with your reader. If you review the events in your life carefully, you will find many such experiences worth relating. Topics of current public interest being discussed in newspapers and magazines and on radio and television also provide excellent material for student writing. If such a topic stirs your interest, investigate it further; your classmates will probably share this interest and would like to know your opinions on the subject.

A procedure you may find helpful when you have difficulty in selecting a subject is simply to sit down and begin writing whatever comes into your head. Experts on creativity say that even if you do not have the vaguest idea for a topic when you begin, the mere act of putting ideas on paper in a free-association process releases creative energy. After you have jotted down as much as you can on paper, look over what you have written. Very likely you will discover a topic there that can be developed into an interesting theme. Of course, much will be confused and incoherent at this point; but as you explore the possibilities of a topic, you can rearrange, reorder, analyze, and classify until what you have written makes sense. You can then eliminate the irrelevant and begin building an outline.

EXERCISE 18

A. Think back over your own experiences, and make a list of ten to fifteen subjects that could be used as theme topics. Select those experiences that provided you with an insight into life.

1._____
2._____
3._____
4._____
5._____
6._____
7._____
8._____
9._____
10._____
11._____
12._____
13._____
14._____
15._____

B. Peruse several newspapers and weekly news magazines for a few days, and make notes of current topics that you would like to write about. List ten of them below.

1._____
2._____
3._____
4._____
5._____
6._____
7._____
8._____
9._____
10._____

2. NARROWING THE TOPIC

The problem of narrowing your topic is not so crucial if you have been assigned a specific topic. However, if you are allowed to choose your own subject, or if the assigned topic is rather broad, you should restrict it to one you can handle within the length of the paper you intend to write. For example, your instructor may ask you to write an impromptu 300-word theme in class, or may assign a 700-word paper to be written out of class. This stipulation of length is not designed to make you produce an exact number of words: it is meant rather to define the scope of your subject. The shorter your paper, the more you will have to restrict your topic.

Let us assume that you are assigned a 500-word theme on a subject of your own choice and that you decide to write on college sports. You could write 500 words on college sports by presenting an overview of the subject, moving rapidly from one large aspect to another. In successive paragraphs you might deal with the types of sports offered on a college campus, their respective requirements for participation, the general value of participation to the student, and so on. But this kind of treatment would be too general to arouse much interest. By rejecting such a broad topic in favor of a more limited one, such as "Volleyball: No Game for Softies" or "The Value of Intramural Sports," you can reduce the scope of your subject to a topic that can be successfully managed in 500 words. Not having so much ground to cover, you could develop each point in greater detail and produce a much more interesting paper.

In selecting your topic, then, consider carefully the proposed length of your paper. You might begin with a broad subject to discover how much you know about it, but as you proceed, you will need to focus on one aspect of it. The character of your intended audience will also affect your choice of subject. You can expect an audience of your fellow English students to understand and respond to a lively discussion of some topic of current public interest or an account of a personal experience. But they are not likely to understand or be interested in a technical explanation of some complicated engineering process. For example, a paper on the importance of desalting ocean water to satisfy the world's growing need for water is more suitable than a detailed, scientific discussion of the desalinization process.

EXERCISE 19

A. Consider these items as possible subjects for a 500-word theme. Some are too broad for such an assignment; after these write *too broad*. Some are too technical; after these write *too technical*. And some are suitable; after these write *satisfactory*.

1. sociology _____

2. Congressional committees _____

3. guerrilla warfare _____

4. sexual mutations in the tsetse fly _____

5. the care and cleaning of the 155 millimeter howitzer _____

6. my favorite employer _____

7. the used car as a status symbol _____

8. heating swimming pools with solar power _____

9. shooting underwater pictures _____

10. violence in American life _____

B. These subjects are too general to be covered in a short theme. Select five that interest you and divide each into three subtopics, each a suitable subject for a 300- to 500-word theme.

1. government

_____

_____

_____

2. prejudices

_____

_____

_____

3. new sources of energy

_____

_____

_____

4. ecology

_____

_____

_____

5. race relations in the United States

_____

_____

_____

6. pets

_____

_____

_____

7. economics

_____

_____

_____

8. sports

_____

_____

_____

9. architecture

_____

_____

_____

10. agriculture

_____

_____

_____

3. THINKING THROUGH THE TOPIC

Having chosen your topic and limited it to something you can handle in the space available, you must consider carefully just what you want to say about it. You may have a definite purpose in mind before you begin to organize your thoughts. More often, you may not be able to formulate your aim until you have collected and organized your material in some detail. But whether you establish your purpose early or evolve it as you work out the plan of your paper, you will find it helpful at this stage to spend some time thinking about your general intention, about what you want your reader to get from reading your paper. This preliminary thinking will often give you a framework for your ideas and so minimize the frustrations of getting started.

4. GATHERING AND ORGANIZING MATERIAL

Composing a theme, like composing a paragraph, demands careful attention to supporting detail. Because of its greater length, a theme requires more facts, illustrations, and judgments to support its ideas; and it takes time to accumulate this material. When you are given a week to prepare a paper, therefore, do not wait until the night before the paper is due to begin thinking about supporting materials, but begin gathering them immediately.

Materials for writing come from a variety of sources — from personal experiences, lectures, class discussions, campus bull sessions, books, magazines, newspapers, and so forth. When writing an essay examination, you will depend largely on the experiences and ideas of others — on lecture notes, on notes of your readings, and on your own thoughts about what you have heard and read. When writing a theme on a personal experience, however, you will have to rely on your own feelings and attitudes for ideas.

As many experienced students will tell you, a good way to organize your ideas for an essay to be written in class (under pressure or within a limited time period) is to work up a brief informal outline of your thoughts before you begin to write. Begin with the major ideas, the ideas that will serve as the topic sentences of your paragraphs, and then supply a few supporting details under each main heading. An informal outline of an essay on the disadvantages of a college student's owning an automobile might look something like this:

Parking and traffic problem
　Parking spaces during popular class hours scarce
　Tardiness and absences because of traffic jams
Expense of operation
　Initial cost—financing and depreciation
　Insurance
　Upkeep
Interference with studies
　Part-time job to keep up payments reduces study time
　Maintenance costs cut into educational supplies budget

This kind of scratch outline need not be very elaborate. Its function is simply to help you to organize your thoughts before you begin to write. The short time it takes to prepare is amply justified by the improvement it will make in the coherence and unity of your writing. Having established a framework for your thoughts, you can devote more attention to their lucid and precise expression.

A paper written out of class can be developed in greater detail. For example, if you were given a week to write a paper on the characteristics of good college teachers, you might begin by listing the ideas obtained from your reading as well as those derived from your own experience. Your list would probably contain irrelevant and awkwardly phrased items, but this is not important at this stage. The important thing is to get your ideas down on paper so that you will not forget them before you begin to write. Your preliminary listing of detail might develop in this manner:

1. Praises student achievement
2. Has patience
3. Accepts student limitations and range of abilities
4. Knows subject
5. Sense of humor
6. Love of subject
7. Does not patronize, talk down to students
8. Command of language—expresses thoughts clearly
9. Keeps abreast of developments in his field
10. Provides interesting illuminating material in lectures rather than a rehash of text
11. Considerate, tactful—can accept opposing views
12. Does not simply read lectures but asks questions, leads discussion
13. Prepares well, structures course
14. Stimulates student interest in subject by his or her own enthusiasm

15. Good teachers need more recognition
16. Brings in material of current interest
17. Students differ in their opinions
18. Knows related fields
19. Good teachers are popular
20. Frequently brings in interesting books from his or her own library to recommend
21. Continues study of subject matter on his or her own
22. Provides additional help when asked — cheerfully

Grouping related items and discarding irrelevant ones is the next step. The items in the list above might be grouped under the following main headings:

Attitude toward students
    Praises student achievement (1)
    Has patience (2)
    Accepts student limitations and range of abilities (3)
    Does not patronize, talk down to students (7)
    Considerate, tactful — can accept opposing views (11)
    Provides additional help when asked — cheerfully (22)
Knowledge of subject
    Keeps abreast of developments in his or her field (9)
    Provides interesting, illuminating material in lectures rather than a rehash of text (10)
    Knows related fields (18)
Love of subject
    Stimulates student interest in subject by his or her own enthusiasm (14)
    Frequently brings in interesting books from his or her own library to recommend (20)
    Continues study of subject matter on his or her own (21)
Class presentation
    Sense of humor (5)
    Command of language — expresses thoughts clearly (8)
    Does not simply read lectures but asks questions, leads discussion (12)
    Prepares well, structures course (13)

The grouping of detail in this preliminary outline is somewhat arbitrary. A sense of humor (item 5), for example, might illustrate an attitude toward students as well as serve as a device to enliven classroom presentation. Note also that items 15, 16, 17, and 19 have been eliminated. Item 16 repeats number 10; and items 15, 17, and 19 — that good teachers deserve more recognition, that students have different ideas on what makes a good teacher, and that good teachers are popular—are not relevant to a discussion of the qualities of a good teacher.

As you look over your groupings, you may discover that one heading contains many more items than any other. If this occurs, you may decide to write on the subject of that heading rather than on your original subject. Shifting your attention to your new subject, you could then supply additional detail and organize it in the same manner as you did the original topic. This possibility illustrates an important fact about an outline: it is not irrevocable. It is only a means to an end; and when you modify your purpose, you can modify your outline accordingly.

After you have completed this grouping, you must arrange your major and minor ideas in some effective order. The order you use will depend on the nature of your materials and on your purpose (see pp. 87–91). For an expository theme such as this one, an order of climax is usually effective. Examining your ideas, you may decide that a teacher's positive attitude is the most important attribute of a good teacher and so place this idea last for emphasis. You may also decide that knowledge of subject is next in importance and place this idea at the beginning to give it secondary emphasis. Arranging the ideas in a climactic order yields the following informal outline:

A. Knowledge of subject
    1. Keeps abreast of developments in his or her field (9)
    2. Knows related fields (18)
    3. Provides interesting, illuminating material in lectures rather than a rehash of text (10)
B. Love of subject
    1. Continues study of subject matter on his or her own (21)
    2. Stimulates student interest in subject by his or her own enthusiasm (14)
A. 3. Frequently brings in interesting books from his or her own library to recommend (20)
C. Class presentation
    1. Command of language—expresses thoughts clearly (8)
    2. Does not simply read lectures but asks questions, leads discussion (12)
    3. Prepares well, structures course (13)
    4. Sense of humor (5)
D. Attitude toward students
    1. Considerate, tactful—can accept opposing views (11)
    2. Has patience (2)
    3. Accepts student limitations and range of abilities (3)

4. Does not patronize, talk down to students (7)
5. Praises student achievement (1)
6. Provides additional help when asked — cheerfully (22)

With this rough outline as a framework for your theme, you can now begin the first draft. You will still have to supply additional clarifying and supporting detail to develop the minor ideas, but this kind of outline provides sufficient direction for a theme of 300 to 500 words. For a longer theme a more fully developed, formal outline is often required.

EXERCISE 20

A. Select one of the specific topics you listed in Exercise 18A, 18B, or 19B, and supply several facts, ideas, and illustrations gathered from your own reflections or from your reading that you might use to develop it.

TOPIC_____

Detail   1._____

         2._____

         3._____

         4._____

         5._____

         6._____

         7._____

         8._____

         9._____

       10._____

       11._____

       12._____

B. In each of the following groups, one idea could serve as a major heading for the other ideas. Identify the major heading and write it in the blanks provided.

1. professional basketball players average more than $100,000 a year; quarterbacks on football teams are paid as much as $250,000 a year; Jim "Catfish" Hunter signed a contract for more than $3,000,000; several tennis professionals' earnings are in the six figures bracket; hockey players are handsomely paid; professional athletes earn high salaries

Main Heading _____

2. subject to abuse from newspaper columnists; disadvantages of a politician's life; frequently blamed for adverse economic conditions over which they have no control; target of unstable cranks; work physically and emotionally draining; long hours away from home campaigning; little job security

Main Heading _____

3. excellent body-conditioning exercise; satisfying recreational activity; values of learning to swim; protection against drowning; prolongs life

Main Heading _____

4. reduce intake of refined sugar; keep body weight down; moderate intake of coffee and liquor; don't smoke; avoid consistently high intake of fatty foods; keeping fit; eat a balanced diet; get a physical examination once a year after thirty-five years of age

Main Heading _____

5. study question carefully; make scratch outline of important points; think before you write; useful advice when writing an essay examination; support main ideas with adequate factual detail, illustrations, or reasons; take care with punctuation, spelling, grammatical constructions

Main Heading _____

C. Arrange the following items under three main headings. One of the items will serve as a title, another as a thesis statement (the statement that expresses the main point).

1. An educated person should know a little about everything and a lot about something.
2. A vision of the good life is needed.
3. The ability to recognize specious reasoning, phony arguments.
4. Reinforcement of moral virtues — courage, integrity, compassion, honor — are provided by a good education.
5. The qualities of an educated person.
6. The corruption of personal honor ultimately corrupts society.
7. A well-educated person is a harmonious blend of intellectual, moral, and emotional capacities.
8. Mastery of self-expression is basic in speaking and in writing.
9. When uncontrolled, the emotions can paralyze, disorient, and isolate people.
10. Knowledge in the major categories of learning is required — humanities, social sciences, natural sciences.
11. An educated person is not only willing to listen to others, but is willing to take a stand.
12. An understanding of the disruptive power of the emotions is needed.
13. To think clearly requires the ability to formulate a persuasive argument and to follow one presented by someone else.
14. A good education gives one knowledge about and experience in controlling one's emotions.
15. Intellectual capacity means a well-stocked, flexible mind as well as a mind capable of thinking clearly and expressing itself clearly.
16. Development of emotional stability is a third requirement.
17. A well-educated person is less a victim of uncontrolled passions.
18. A human being is more an emotional than a rational animal.

Title _____

THESIS STATEMENT _____

_____

a. _____

_____

_____

_____

_____

_____

b. _____

_____

_____

_____

c. _____

_____

_____

_____

_____

_____

D. Select a subject from the following list, narrow it, and write out three or four main ideas that could be used to develop it.

1. clothing fashions
2. automobile design
3. my home town
4. educational innovation
5. recreational activities
6. marriage in the modern world
7. mental therapy
8. terrorism
9. tourism
10. disappearing wildlife

GENERAL SUBJECT _____

SPECIFIC SUBJECT _____

Main Idea a. _____

b. _____

c. _____

d. _____

5. OUTLINING

The kind of rough outline described in the preceding section is usually sufficient for a theme of 300 to 500 words. For a longer, more complex writing assignment, however, you will find it helpful to make a more detailed, formal outline. The longer paper requires more careful preparation; it requires you to work out the relationships and the development of your thoughts more thoroughly. And a formal outline forces you to do just this. Beginning writers sometimes neglect the outline because of the time required to prepare it. But, as you will discover, the more time you spend in carefully preparing your outline, the less time you will waste when you begin to write. With a clearly detailed plan of your theme before you, you will not have to grope for ideas to clarify and develop your thesis.

An outline has three parts: the *title*, the *thesis statement*, and the *body*. The body consists of the major and minor ideas that develop the main idea of the outline expressed in the thesis statement. The main ideas are represented by Roman numerals, minor ideas by capital letters, Arabic numerals, and lower case letters, as illustrated in the following system:

I.
　A.
　　1.
　　　a.
　　　(1)
　　　　(a)

Each main heading (I, II, etc.) need not be developed in as much detail as this illustration. An outline for a theme of 300 to 500 words usually does not require subdivision beyond the first Arabic numerals.

I.
　A.
　　1.
　　2.
　B.
II.

Capitalize the first word of each heading, and if the heading is a sentence place a period at the end. Occasionally the entries on a sentence outline may extend to two or three lines. When they do, make certain that your left-hand margin does not extend to the left of the period after the topic symbol, as illustrated below.

I. _____

   A. _____

     _____

     _____

The thesis statement appears between the title and the first Roman numeral.

Title

THESIS STATEMENT _____

_____

I. _____

The thesis statement expresses the controlling idea of your paper. Written just above the first entry of the outline, it serves as a visible guide, a reminder of your main idea so that you can prevent irrelevant material from creeping into your outline.

Your thesis statement should be as precise as you can make it. The more sharply focused it is, the more it will help you in clarifying and developing your thought. For example, "There are several advantages in using a checking account" is not as useful a thesis statement as the more precise, "A checking account provides a convenient and safe method of payment." The latter statement forces the writer to consider each idea and thus ensures a fuller, more specific development of the central idea. If you decide to add or delete items in your outline, revise your thesis statement to reflect any change in your main idea. For example, in developing an outline on the advantages of paying by check, if you decide to discuss the disadvantages as well, you can change your thesis statement accordingly.

The most frequently used forms of the outline are the *topic outline* and the *sentence outline*. The entries on a topic outline are made up of short phrases or single words. The following exemplifies a topic outline:

Violence in School: A Growing Problem in the United States

THESIS STATEMENT   The increase in school violence in Ameri-

can schools is creating serious financial and educational problems for
school districts.

I. Nature of problem
   A. Abuse of students
      1. Physical assaults
         a. Beatings
         b. Rape
         c. Murder
      2. Mental and emotional harassment
   B. Attacks on teachers and school board members
   C. Vandalism of school property
II. Response by school authorities
   A. Increased use of armed guards
      1. Off-duty policemen in Chicago
      2. District-employed patrols in Los Angeles
   B. Increased use of hardware
      1. Laser-beam alarm signals
      2. Walkie-talkies for teachers
      3. Police helicopters
III. Consequence of increasing violence
   A. Depletion of school budgets
      1. Less money for supplies and facilities
      2. Less money for maintenance
      3. Less money for teaching staff
   B. Adverse effect on student learning
   C. Community anger at lack of safety in schools
      1. Attacks on school board members
      2. Lack of financial support for school bonds
IV. Solutions to problem
   A. Hard-line approach
      1. Increased use of armed guards and police
      2. Swift apprehension of offenders
      3. Jail and prison sentences for juveniles
   B. Long-term approach
      1. Reduction of violence in mass media
      2. Improvement in lives of underprivileged
      3. Restructuring of schools to ease competition and tensions
   C. Other approaches
      1. More vocational education
      2. Reductions in class size
      3. Release of unmotivated students
      4. Alternative of community service instead of jail for
         offenders

5. New rights and responsibilities for students to aid in control of violence

In a sentence outline each entry is a sentence.

Study Suggestions

THESIS STATEMENT   An effective method for absorbing the material of a reading assignment involves four steps: previewing the assignment, reading the assignment, reviewing the assignment, and reciting the main points.

I. Before you begin to read, preview the assignment.
   A. Make certain of the exact pages to be read.
   B. Read the opening and closing paragraphs.
   C. Examine the major and minor divisions of the selection.
   D. Study the pictures, charts, maps, and so forth that illustrate important points.
II. After this preliminary survey, read the assignment carefully.
   A. Underline the important ideas.
   B. Look up the meaning of unfamiliar words.
   C. Place question marks after statements that need further clarification or support.
III. Review the assignment.
   A. Reread introductory and summary passages.
   B. Analyze the structure of the selection.
      1. Distinguish between major and minor ideas and relate each to the central thesis.
      2. Distinguish between the statement of an idea and an illustration of it.
      3. Consider cause and effect relationships.
IV. Fix the main points in your memory.
   A. Make notes of the structure and important ideas of the selection.
   B. Recite the main points to yourself.
   C. Discuss your interpretation of the author's thought with your classmates.
   D. Relate the information presented in the assignment to that presented in a preceding chapter by the same author or to the ideas of another writer on the same subject.

Of the two forms, the topic outline is generally easier to manage, but because the theme itself will be composed of sentences, the sentence outline provides a more convenient basis than the topic outline for the translation of thought from outline to theme.

If you are to do an effective job of outlining, you must know some-thing of the principles that govern the construction of an outline as well as its format. These concern (1) logical subordination of ideas, (2) parallel structure, (3) single subdivisions, and (4) specific, mean-ingful headings. The most important of these principles is the first, for the main purpose of your outline is to give you a logical, well-organized structure for your composition. Examine your outline first to be sure that your main headings are logical divisions of the subject expressed in the title and thesis statement. Make certain that the subheadings are logical divisions of the headings under which they are listed. Study the following outline for logical organization and subordination of ideas:

The Ecological Importance of Open Space

THESIS STATEMENT   Open space is essential to the maintenance of a healthful, life-supporting environment.

  I. Open space plays a vital role in maintaining breathable air.
     A. Open space vegetation filters particles from the air.
     B. It produces oxygen through the process of photosyn-thesis.
 II. Urban areas produce the elements of smog.
III. Intelligent use of open space can help to maintain a healthful climate.
     A. Open space dissipates islands of heat produced in urban areas.
        1. Covered surfaces, such as asphalt, absorb heat.
        2. Urban areas produce heat through combustion.
     B. Native vegetation of open space helps to reduce humidity built up in the cities and suburbs.
        1. Water needed for exotic plants in urban and suburban communities increases water evaporation.
IV. Invasion of open space by urban and suburban sprawl impairs its recreational use.
     A. Open space surrounding cities is often used by city-dwell-ing hikers and cyclists.
     B. Housing tracts and shopping centers occupy space that could be better used for public parks and campgrounds near densely populated cities.
  V. Wildlife, essential to a healthful ecological system, is threat-ened by the elimination of open space.
 VI. Empty beach land should be purchased by a state or the fed-eral government and preserved for recreational use.

VII. The movement of population from rural to urban areas has increased urban congestion.

Some of the main headings of this outline are not logical divisions of the subject. Roman numeral II should be placed under I, VI should be worked into IV, and VII should be eliminated. Item III, B, 1 also needs to be absorbed into B. Revising the outline to correct these errors results in a more logical arrangement:

I. Open space plays a vital role in maintaining breathable air.
   A. Open space vegetation filters particles from the air.
   B. It produces oxygen through the process of photosynthesis.
   C. Automobiles and factories in urban areas produce smog.
II. Intelligent use of open space can help to maintain a healthful climate.
   A. Open space dissipates islands of heat produced in urban areas.
      1. Covered surfaces, such as asphalt, absorb heat.
      2. Urban areas produce heat through combustion.
   B. Native vegetation of open space helps to reduce humidity produced by evaporation of water used to irrigate exotic plants in cities and suburbs.
III. Invasion of open space by urban and suburban sprawl impairs its recreational use.
   A. Open space surrounding cities is often used by city-dwelling hikers and cyclists.
   B. Housing tracts and shopping centers occupy space that could be better used for public parks and campgrounds near densely populated cities.
   C. Empty beach land should be purchased by a state or the federal government and preserved for recreational use.
IV. Wildlife, essential to a healthful ecological system, is threatened by the elimination of open space.

The principle of parallelism, which requires that ideas of equal importance in a sentence be expressed in the same grammatical form, applies to the construction of outlines. An outline is parallel when the headings designated by the same kind of letter or numeral are phrased in parallel form. That is, if Roman numeral I is a prepositional phrase, the other Roman numerals should be prepositional phrases also. If A and B under I are nouns, so must be the other capital letters under II, III, and so on. A sentence outline is automatically parallel, for each entry is a sentence and hence parallel. The following outline is not parallel:

A Part-time Job for the College Student

I. Pays for college expenses
   A. Tuition
   B. Books
   C. For supplies
   D. Recreation
II. It provides a student with vocational training.
   A. He learns special skills.
   B. Work experience
III. Character development
   A. Self-reliance
   B. Responsibility
   C. Reliability
   D. Cooperation

None of the major headings of this outline are parallel: Roman numeral I is a verb phrase, II is a sentence, and III is a noun phrase. The capital letter entries illustrate the same flaw. Item C under I is a prepositional phrase, whereas the other items are nouns. Under II, A is a sentence, and B is a noun phrase. When these errors are corrected, the outline is more consistent. The ideas are presented more effectively.

A Part-time Job for the College Student

I. Helps to pay for college expenses
   A. Tuition
   B. Books
   C. Supplies
   D. Recreation
II. Provides student with vocational training
   A. Skills
   B. Experience
III. Develops student's character
   A. Self-reliance
   B. Responsibility
   C. Reliability
   D. Cooperation

The basis of outlining, as we have seen, is the division of larger topics into smaller ones. When you divide a topic into its parts, you must, logically, have at least two parts. In constructing an outline, therefore, avoid the single subdivision. If you divide a Roman numeral heading, you must have at least an A and a B under it. If you divide a capital letter heading, you must provide at least a 1 and a 2 under it, and so on through each successive stage of the outline. Consider the following outline:

The Benefits of Participation in Sports

I. Pleasure of competition
II. Value of exercise
III. Development of character
    A. Sportsmanship
IV. Interest and skill in a recreational activity

Item A under III represents only one division of a larger topic, development of character. If the writer wished to emphasize character development by analyzing it in greater detail than the other topics, he should have provided at least two subdivisions of this heading. If, however, he simply wanted to emphasize this one aspect of character development, he should have incorporated it in his main heading. These two possibilities are illustrated below:

I. Pleasure of competition
II. Value of exercise
III. Development of character
    A. Sportsmanship
    B. Cooperation
    C. Self-discipline
IV. Development of interest and skill in a recreational activity

I. Pleasure of competition
II. Value of exercise
III. Development of good sportsmanship
IV. Development of interest and skill in a recreational activity

Finally, make certain that your outline headings convey specific, meaningful ideas. General headings such as "introduction," "body," "conclusion," or "examples," "functions," "types," and the like do not represent the subject matter of an outline very clearly and therefore provide little guidance when you translate the ideas from your outline to the composition.

After you have completed your outline, examine it carefully to see that its format is correct and that the organization of its ideas is logical and consistent. Be sure that you have included a title and a thesis statement and that you have used symbols correctly and consistently. As you check the body of the outline, make certain that you have avoided single subdivisions and vague, meaningless headings and that entries of the same rank are expressed in parallel structure. If your outline meets these tests, you are ready to begin your first draft.

EXERCISE 21

A. Compose a precise, accurate thesis statement for an outline based on the material concerning a good college teacher that was presented in section 4, "Gathering and Organizing Material" (pp. 186–89).

B. Use the detail in the following groups of sentences to phrase a concise, comprehensive thesis statement for an outline on the subject. Write your thesis statement in the blanks provided.

1. (1) College education demands that students be capable of expressing themselves. (2) They must be able to read carefully and write clearly. (3) They must be able to speak their thoughts and listen attentively. (4) College students must be able to handle language if they are to succeed in college.

THESIS STATEMENT _____

_____

2. (1) In the Netherlands Moluccan terrorists killed several people aboard a Dutch train to publicize their demands for independence for their former homeland. (2) The Basques in northern Spain want a Basque state independent of France and Spain. (3) Scottish nationalists seek independence from England, and in France Brittany has both a right- and left-wing movement that seeks to establish a separate Breton state. (4) And, of course, separatist sentiment can be found among the Flemish in Belgium.

THESIS STATEMENT _____

_____

3. (1) Cuba provides Russia with a base for operations in the Caribbean Sea. (2) The establishment of normal diplomatic relations between the United States and Cuba is not likely to reduce Cuba's economic dependence on the Soviet Union. (3) Cuba has gradually become a replica of the Soviet police state. (4) Resumption of relations with Cuba would indicate American acceptance of the permanence of the Communist government in Cuba.

THESIS STATEMENT _____

_____

4. (1) Reading enables people to broaden their interests and to learn about life in foreign lands, ages, and cultures. (2) The ability to read is a requirement for most interesting jobs. (3) Reading provides a useful, convenient, enjoyable pastime. (4) Reading ability is essential for citizens in a democracy, who need to keep themselves informed on important issues in order to vote intelligently. (5) Lack of reading ability is a serious intellectual, psychological, and cultural handicap.

THESIS STATEMENT _____

_____

5. (1) Anxious extroverts have their hands continually in the air to answer questions. (2) They are never satisfied unless they can add their thoughts to the discussion. (3) The campus lover answers a question occasionally but is more interested in the cute blonde on the right than in what goes on in class. (4) Some students never volunteer an opinion or an answer. (5) They sit there the whole semester, content to let others carry the discussion. (6) Classroom discussions evoke different reactions in students.

THESIS STATEMENT _____

_____

C. The outline below contains many of the defects explained and illustrated in the preceding pages. Study each entry carefully, and if it illustrates one of the following errors, write its number in the appropriate space. Be prepared to explain how you would correct the error.

1. item not placed under the logical heading _____

_____

2. item not parallel in form with other headings of equal rank _____

_____

3. heading vague and meaningless _____

_____

4. single subdivision of a heading _____

_____

Tips for New Students

THESIS STATEMENT   To make their adjustment to college as smooth as possible, new students should give a good deal of thought to their course of study, living quarters, orientation-week procedures, regular study routine, and reasonable social diversion.

  I. Selection of course of study (1)
    A. Consultation with counselor (2)
      1. Aptitude tests (3)
      2. Consider your high-school record (4)
    B. Study of college catalog (5)
    C. Experts (6)
 II. Choice of living quarters (7)
    A. Residence on campus (8)
      1. Types (9)
      2. Fraternities and sororities (10)
      3. Dormitories (11)
    B. Residence off campus (12)
      1. Apartments in town (13)
    C. Rooms in private houses in town (14)

III. Need for orientation and preparation (15)
  A. Tour the campus to discover the location of important buildings (16)
  B. Familiarity with registration procedure (17)
  C. Familiarity with schedule (18)
  D. Purchase of books and supplies (19)
IV. Importance of regular study routine (20)
  A. Necessity of established daily study hours (21)
  B. Completion of assignments on time (22)
 V. Value of social activities (23)
  A. Need for relaxation and recreation (24)
  B. Development of poise and self-confidence (25)
    1. School dances (26)
VI. Conclusion (27)

D. Reconstruct the outline in C above to correct its format. Add whatever details are necessary.

E. Material for an outline on the supersonic transport Concorde is listed below. Organize the items into a topic or sentence outline, and write your headings in the appropriate blanks in the outline following this list. Construct a thesis statement for your outline as well as a title.

1. A more serious problem with the Concorde, however, is that it is uneconomical to operate.
2. The engines of the Concorde are about the same size as those of the 747, but they are much noisier.
3. The ozone layer protects the earth against dangerous dosages of ultraviolet radiation.
4. Serious objections have been raised by environmentalists.
5. The cost of operation will be high also.
6. The Concorde carries fewer passengers (100 to 125) than the 747 (350 to 400).
7. Environmentalists object to the noise level of the Concorde.
8. The cost of development of the Concorde has come to more than $3 billion.
9. On takeoff the Concorde is about three times as loud as the B707, and the B707 is one of the loudest of the subsonic jets.
10. The Concorde fares will have to exceed by as much as 20 percent first-class fares on subsonic jet transports.
11. Jet noise is proportional to the velocity of the exhaust.
12. The velocity of exhaust in the Concorde is higher because its engines must operate at higher altitudes where the air is thinner.
13. Operating at lower altitudes, the 747 can use the high-bypass turbojet engine that has a lower exhaust velocity and is therefore quieter.
14. The increase in the price of fuel during the past four years has also increased the cost of operation beyond the projected amount.
15. France hoped that the Concorde would help Europe compete against American dominance in commercial air transportation.

16. The likely failure of the Concorde will not ease French frustrations here.
17. Environmentalists also fear that the emission of nitric oxides in the exhaust of the Concorde will break down the ozone layer of the stratosphere.
18. It seems unlikely that more than sixteen will ever be built at a cost of $60 million each.
19. Only nine have been purchased so far, and the French and British governments have been the purchasers.
20. The Concorde may well upset, at least temporarily, American relations with Britain and France.
21. If the United States does not grant landing rights, Britain and France may well retaliate against the United States in other fields.
22. A breakdown in the ozone layer could increase the incidence of skin cancer caused by ultraviolet radiation.
23. Some observers believe that Britain and France secretly want the United States to refuse landing rights for the Concorde to give them a scapegoat for their lack of success with the plane.
24. The French may well see American opposition as jealousy over a superior technological achievement.

Title _____

THESIS STATEMENT _____

_____

I. _____

   A. _____

      1. _____

         a. _____

         b. _____

         c. _____

      2. _____

   B. _____

      1. _____

      2. _____

II. _____

   A. _____

      1. _____

      2. _____

   B. _____

      1. _____

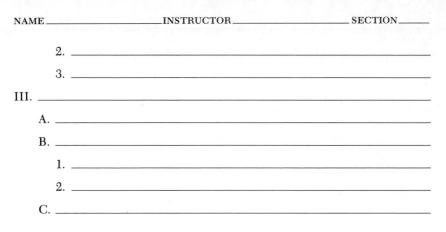

2. _____

3. _____

III. _____

   A. _____

   B. _____

     1. _____

     2. _____

   C. _____

F. Compose a sentence outline on a subject listed in one of the following exercises: 18A, 18B, 19B, 20D.

6. WRITING THE FIRST DRAFT

Once you have completed the outline, you are ready to begin the first draft of your paper. Your outline provides the plan, the framework, of your paper. Now you must transform this plan into the finished structure.

The major headings of an outline will coincide with the main ideas of the composition, but there is not an exact correspondence between the main headings of the outline and the paragraphs of the composition. A Roman numeral heading may require one or more paragraphs for adequate development, depending on the amount of detail it encompasses. The first main heading of the outline "Violence in School: A Growing Problem in the United States" (pp. 196–98)

    I. Nature of problem
       A. Abuse of students
       B. Attacks on teachers and school board members
       C. Vandalism of school property

would require at least a paragraph but possibly two or three for full development. Conversely, in a short composition, two Roman numeral headings might be included in one paragraph.

Plan your time so that you can revise your first draft carefully. Once you begin the first draft, move steadily forward. Do not worry about mechanics at this stage. The important thing is to get your ideas on paper. You can correct errors in spelling, punctuation, and grammar and make improvements in wording later, when you revise this draft. If you stop to check these items now, you may lose your train of thought.

EXERCISE 22

A. Write a first draft of a theme based on the outline you developed for Exercise 20C, 21E, or 21F.

B. Write a first draft of a theme based on the outline concerning the characteristics of a good college teacher that was presented in section 4, "Gathering and Organizing Material" (pp. 188–89).

7. REVISING THE FIRST DRAFT

Do not begin to revise your first draft immediately after you have completed it. Set it aside for several hours (overnight if possible) and think about something else. When you return to your paper, your mind will be clearer and fresher, and you will be able to view the first draft more objectively.

In your revision, concentrate first on the content and organization of your ideas. Read your paragraphs carefully to make certain that they are unified, well developed, and coherent. The following suggestions, which were discussed in the first four chapters, should be helpful.

Content and Organization

Unity The controlling idea of each paragraph should be clearly and concisely stated in a topic sentence. Each sentence of the paragraph should support this idea.

Development Each paragraph should contain enough detail— enough facts, illustrations, comparisons, and judgments—to explain the controlling idea adequately. The supporting detail should be concrete and specific. Every generalization should be supported by sufficient evidence to persuade a fair-minded reader.

Coherence The ideas in each paragraph should be arranged in a logical sequence. The sentences in each paragraph, as well as the paragraphs themselves, should flow smoothly together.

The last suggestion regarding coherence needs further comment. Our previous discussion of coherence concentrated on coherence *within* the paragraph. When you write a longer composition, you must make certain that the thought flows smoothly *between* paragraphs as well as between sentences. If you have organized your paper carefully, there should be a steady development of thought from paragraph to paragraph, but you can accentuate this continuity through judicious use of transitional expressions and through repetition of key words. In the following passage, for example, the writer uses both these devices to ensure continuity between paragraphs:

> Even the shift in the kind of curriculum is upsetting. The students are used to having the day arranged for them from, say, nine to three, high-school fashion. They now find themselves attending classes for only fifteen hours or so a week. The concentration in depth on a few subjects is a new idea to them. The requisite self-

discipline is often something they learn only after painful experience.

Furthermore, college is the students' first encounter with live intellectuals. They meet individual members of the faculty who have written important books or completed important pieces of research. The various intellectual fields become matters of personal experience. The students learn that work does not just happen to get done. They find that the productive intellectual is not a superman but an everyday figure. They will also make the discovery that there are those who consider intellectual pursuits reason enough for an entire life. Students are nearly always surprised to find such pursuits valued so highly.

Students are surprised, too, at their first meeting with really violent political opinion. . . . [From James K. Feibleman, "What Happens in College," *Saturday Review*, October 20, 1962.]

Furthermore, the first word of the second paragraph, informs us that the writer is adding another illustration of the idea he has been developing in the preceding paragraph. The transition between the second and third paragraphs is especially smooth.

. . . Students are nearly always surprised to find such pursuits valued so highly.
Students are surprised, too, at their first meeting . . .

The repetition of the word *students* in the latter sentence plus the use of the transitional *too*, which signals an additional illustration of the author's point in the preceding two paragraphs, provides an uninterrupted bridge of thought as we move from one paragraph to the next. The repetition of key words such as *students* and its pronoun *they* throughout the passage also ties the paragraphs together.

Emphasis

After you have tested your paper for unity, development, and coherence, examine it once more to make certain you have given your most important ideas the proper emphasis. To make your reader receptive to the effect you wish to create, you must communicate your thoughts clearly and forcefully. The most emphatic positions in a composition are the beginning and the end. Reread your opening and closing sentences. Now is the time to revise and polish these sentences. What you say in the opening sentence often determines the kind of reading your paper will receive. If your first sentence successfully arouses the interest and curiosity of your readers, they will probably give your paper a sympathetic reading. If it is rather dull and colorless, their reading will probably be more perfunctory. The first few sentences are especially important if the purpose of your paper is to argue a point. In this case you must establish yourself as a reasonable individual, not as a fanatic. If your introduction makes a reader suspicious or uneasy about your motives, it will be difficult to persuade him of anything.

What you say in the closing sentence is even more important. You can regain your readers' interest after an uninspiring introduction with lively material in the body of the paper, but you have no second chance after they have finished reading. What your readers read last, they usually remember best. If your last sentence is vague and inconclusive, their final impression is not apt to be favorable. Read over your first draft carefully, therefore, and revise your opening and closing sentences to make them as effective as possible. The following discussion will provide some specific suggestions for opening and closing sentences.

Beginning the Paper

A paper longer than 500 words may require an introductory paragraph to introduce its subject and explain its purpose, but for most short themes the first paragraph can both introduce the subject and develop the first main idea. Whether your introduction is a single sentence or a whole paragraph, however, begin with a sentence that is interesting and says something important about the subject.

There are a number of ways to begin a composition. Occasionally you may wish to shock your reader with a *startling statistic* or a *bold statement:*

Two of every three people in the world today live on a starvation diet.

In much of the so-called free world, democracy is a fraud.

Or you may attract your reader's attention with an *appropriate quotation:*

No one has bettered the New York *Times'* description of James Fisk, Jr.: "First in war, first in peace and first in the pockets of his countrymen." [From *Time*, February 23, 1959, p. 104.]

"When I hear the word *culture* I reach for my revolver," said the late Marshal Goering. We all agree he was a barbarian; but, confidentially, when you hear the word *poetry*, do you reach for a mystery story . . . ? [From Gilbert Highet, "Could It Be Verse?" *The Powers of Poetry,* Oxford University Press, 1960.]

A relevant *personal experience* can be effective in tempting a reader:

> I'll never forget one Saturday night when I was a junior in high school and my pals decided to take me to my first burlesque show in downtown Los Angeles. They were all older and taller than I, and I had always felt a bit self-conscious with them, as if I somehow had to prove my manhood to be worthy of their friendship. I wanted to go, but I was a bit nervous for fear I'd reveal my naivete, my innocence. On the way they decided to stop for a beer, and of course I had to drink one, too. As a matter of fact, I drank two, to fortify myself, I suppose. . . .

Quite often a *simple, direct statement of the main idea or purpose* of your paper will be your best choice:

> Good teachers are those who know their subject, love their subject, and are willing and able to share it.

> In this paper I wish to consider Plato's view of an ideal society as he presented it in *The Republic.*

These suggestions do not exhaust the possibilities, of course. As you gain writing experience, you will discover other effective ways to introduce your subject and to elicit reader interest at the same time. As you experiment with different opening statements, keep these suggestions in mind.

First, limit your introduction to one or two sentences, and get directly to the point unless you are writing a long paper. Wandering, irrelevant introductions like the following are deadening:

Why I Want to Be a Doctor

> I guess I've always wanted to be a doctor. My grandfather on my mother's side was a doctor, and I was very fond of Grandad. He used to take me with him on his house calls. . . .

Next, avoid apologizing. A theme that begins "I am not an expert on politics, but . . ." is not likely to arouse much interest.

Third, be wary of the broad generalization as an opener. Statements like "Americans have always envied the Europeans' cultural sophistication" are simply too comprehensive to be supportable. They will not impress an intelligent reader.

Finally, make certain that your first sentence is easily understood without reference to the title. For a theme entitled "Tobacco and the Teen-ager," the following beginning sentence would only confuse the reader: "I guess everybody has tried it by the time he or she is seventeen."

Ending the Paper

For the short theme of 300 to 500 words a special summarizing paragraph is not necessary. A sentence or two is usually sufficient. If your paper is well organized and coherent, your *final detail* will often provide a satisfactory conclusion:

> And, finally, boxing should be banned because of the severe physical damage inflicted on the fighter himself. This result is not surprising, however. In no other sport is it the primary purpose of one contestant to knock his opponent senseless, and it is a rare fighter who can absorb such punishment without suffering serious aftereffects. If it does not kill him — and the possibility is not remote — it may well leave him with the characteristic stumbling shuffle, the thick tongue, the battered face, and the impaired vision of the punch-drunk ex-fighter.

Sometimes, however, you may wish to emphasize your central idea with an apt *quotation:*

> Emerson wrote, "The search after the great man is the dream of youth and the most serious occupation of manhood." Only when people know the best in men will they learn to reject the least in men. The jerks have had their day; it is time now for heroes. [From Marya Mannes, "Let's Stop Exalting Punks," *The Saturday Evening Post*, October 6, 1962, pp. 10–14.]

Or you may refresh your reader's mind by *enumerating the main points* of your paper:

> To answer the usual essay question, then, (1) read the question carefully to determine exactly what is called for; (2) rephrase the question to serve as the central idea of your essay; (3) develop your central idea in one or more paragraphs, using appropriate illustrations, reasons, and factual detail; and (4) organize your paragraphs as you would for an expository or argumentative theme.

A concluding sentence that *repeats the main idea expressed in the opening sentence* can also provide a nice finishing touch:

> Television westerns may provide satisfying entertainment for millions of viewers, but their monotonous plots, stereotyped characters, and simplified themes leave me bored and dissatisfied.

Study the final paragraph of your first draft. If you think a special concluding sentence would add emphasis to your paper, add one. But do not tack on unneeded sentences after you have completed your thought, especially if they contain an apology. An apology at the end of your paper is just as ineffectual as one at the beginning. And do not inject a new idea into your final sentences. A paper that concludes,

> A good climate, expanding job opportunities, abundant recreational areas—all these make Florida a pleasant place to live. One wonders, however, how pleasant it will be as it becomes more crowded.

makes a reader wonder whether the writer has had second thoughts about the validity of his own conclusion.

Proportion

The preceding discussion has stressed the importance of *position* in achieving emphasis. Of equal importance is *proportion,* or balance. In a well-proportioned theme the more important points are given more space; they are developed at greater length. Minor ideas and illustrative detail are not allowed to overshadow or obscure the central thesis. Observe the application of this principle in the following theme:

Democracy on Campus

Perhaps no democratic society has put so much faith in the importance of education as the American. The premise that individuals have a right to the kind of education that will allow them to develop their potential for growth to the fullest is as firmly established in the American mind as the desire for political and religious freedoms. And in few countries of the world has the opportunity for obtaining an education, especially a university education, been made so available to such a large segment of the population. Yet in spite of an almost universal regard for higher education in the United States, recent suggestions calling for fundamental changes in the structure and operation of the American university reveal a basic misunderstanding of the nature of higher education and of the purposes it serves. Particularly misleading, and ultimately dangerous to the welfare of a democracy, is the notion that higher education would be improved if the university were transformed into a truly democratic, quasi-political institution with students and faculty allotted equal power in its governance.

Those who favor a much greater role for students in the administration of a university often argue that students should be treated as full educational partners, that they deserve a representative voice in the educational decisions that affect their lives. They should therefore, so runs the argument, have a say in the selection and retention of faculty, the expenditure of university funds, the determination of course content and grading practices, the kind of research undertaken by faculty, the selection of the president, and so on. Student demands for more power and influence are understandable. The increasing size and impersonality of modern American universities, the emphasis on research to the detriment of good teaching, the general exploitation of undergraduates to finance the more expensive graduate programs—all of these conditions surely indicate that all is not well on American campuses. Students have a right to complain; they do deserve a role in university affairs. But that role should be advisory, not equal to that of the faculty or administration. A university is not a political unit in which power is shared, with students electing their teachers and the administrative officers. It is an educational, a tutorial institution, the function of which is not to govern or rule but to communicate knowledge and cultivate the mind, to transmit the cultural heritage; and it is foolish to speak of democracy in connection with a university's function or operation. Moreover, if students were to be made full partners in the running of a university, they would have to devote much of their time to the process, time that would be taken from their studies, that is, from the work for which they entered the university in the first place.

The conception of the university as a political institution underlies two other demands frequently made in recent years. The first is that the university embark on a program of practical political action to help remedy pressing social problems, and the second, a corollary of the first, that the curriculum be modified or restructured to make courses more "relevant." The proposal that a university engage in political action to ease problems such as poverty, oppression of minorities, slum housing, and the high cost of health care has a certain appeal; for during the past fifty years or so the university has contributed much to improving the quality of life in this country through the work of distinguished university scholars and scientists. The preeminent position of American technology, for example, would have been impossible without the discoveries made by scientists working in university laboratories. The university has also provided many able scholars and experts to advise governmental committees studying the complexities of international trade and foreign policy, and of atomic energy and nuclear disarmament. Although it is legitimate to expect the university to involve itself in important national problems, its role is to study problems and propose solutions, not to engage in partisan politics in support of a cause. When it resorts to such actions, it deserts its traditional moral commitment to objectivity, to the dispassionate consideration of conflicting points of view. Moreover, it invites retaliation from the public on whose support it depends; and when the public loses confidence in the neutrality of the university, it will strip it of its independence, to the detriment of both the university and the public.

The demand that course work be made more relevant to student interests may simply reflect a justifiable desire on the part of students for capable, energetic teachers who are vitally interested in their subject and eager to teach it. But this demand is also made by militant activists, who want to transform the university into a political agency, and by those reluctant to do the hard intellectual labor required of anyone serious about getting an education. The danger to the intellectual integrity of the university were activists' demands to be met has been alluded to above. For the unmotivated, indifferent student, the cry for relevance masks a desire to take up whatever is current, controversial, and popular. It reflects a parochial mind set of those who cannot or will not concentrate on concerns beyond their own immediate needs. Meeting the demands of such students is neither possible nor desirable. On the one hand, it is difficult to keep university courses geared to the latest student interests, since these interests change from one generation of students to another; and on the other hand, trying to keep courses relevant to a student's immediate needs overlooks needs that are not immediately obvious to him but which will be gradually revealed over the years. College study is hard, demanding work, but it is also rewarding to those who approach it with determination and patience. As Jacques Barzun, an eminent historian, reminds us, "What has been acquired with a will is always relevant."

From its beginning in the seventeenth century the American university has contributed immensely to the intellectual, cultural, and economic well-being of this country. In its 240-year history it has helped the American people and their government to meet difficult challenges in a changing world, and in the process it has itself been changed. But it has never abandoned its central concern for the use of and respect for intelligence, so vital to the democratic process. Those who would soften this insistence on intellectual achievement and distinction in hopes of making the university more democratic misunderstand the nature of education as well as the democratic process. Equal opportunity does not mean that all will excel; it means that all should have the chance to excel. If this distinction is blurred, the future of this country will be bleak indeed.

The writer's purpose in this essay is to persuade her reader that the desire to transform the American university into an agency for political action and to restructure its curriculum to keep it relevant to the current interests of its students is unsound. In the first paragraph she introduces the subject and in the last sentence presents the thesis. The second, third, and fourth paragraphs are the longest, for in these paragraphs the writer concentrates on what she judges to be the strongest arguments of the opposition. Surveying the theme as a whole, we can see how she has achieved emphasis through position and proportion. The opening paragraph leads into the subject. The more fully developed middle paragraphs carry the main burden of her case. And the final paragraph, reminding the reader of an important point implied in the beginning paragraph—that equal opportunity when applied to higher education does not guarantee intellectual achievement—concludes the essay forcefully.

Mechanics and Usage

When you are reasonably satisfied with the clarity and organization of your ideas, look over your paper once more to check its mechanics —grammar, punctuation, spelling—diction, and usage. Consult a dictionary or an English handbook whenever necessary as you consider the following questions:

1. Is the meaning of each sentence clear? Are there any dangling or misplaced modifiers, ambiguous pronoun references, or shifts in point of view that cloud the meaning?
2. Is each sentence complete? Are there any sentence fragments, run-together sentences, or sentences with comma splices?
3. Are the sentences correctly punctuated? Are paragraphs properly indented? Are quotation marks used when required?
4. Is each word correctly spelled? Are apostrophes properly placed?
5. Do subjects and verbs, pronouns and antecedents agree?
6. Do the words convey the meaning clearly and precisely? Are emotive terms used justifiably?

EXERCISE 23

A. The following paragraph communicates the writer's idea clearly and forcefully. Examine the opening and closing sentences in particular. What devices does he use to arouse reader interest and to stress his main idea?

Is the sport of hunting, simply as such, a man-worthy thing or isn't it? Let it be supposed that all hunters obey all regulations. Let it be supposed that no whiskey bottle is dropped to pollute any glen or dingle, no fence is broken, no fawn is shot, no forest is set afire, no robins are massacred in mistake for pheasants and no deer-hunters in mistake for porcupines (or possibly chipmunks), and no meditative philosopher, out to enjoy the loveliness of autumn, is ever plugged through the pericardium. The question persists: Is it a spectacle of manhood (which is to say of our distinctive humanness), when on a bracing morning we look out upon the autumn, draw an exhilarating breath, and cry "What a glorious day! How golden in the light of the sun, how merry the caperings of creatures; *Gloria in excelsis Deo!* I will go out and kill something"? [From Alan Devoe, "On Hunting," *American Mercury*, February, 1951. By permission of *The American Mercury*, P. O. Box 1306, Torrance, California 90505.]

B. The following article focuses on one of the most difficult problems facing Americans today: whether their expectations for a better life must be lowered, or whether a solid, sustained economic growth can be achieved without damaging the environment. Read it twice, and on the second reading observe the methods used to provide coherence and emphasis. In particular, note the devices used to link the paragraphs: (1) the use of transitional expressions in the opening sentence of one paragraph to link its thought with that of the preceding paragraph, (2) the repetition of key words, (3) pronoun reference, (4) parallelism, and (5) consistency of point of view. What techniques does the author use to elicit reader interest at the beginning and to emphasize his point at the end?

A Revolution of Disappointed Expectations

One of the most terrifying phenomena to airline pilots is something called wind shear — a situation where an airplane is caught in the convergence of two powerful windstreams moving in opposite directions. The result can be loss of control or disintegration of the plane. And when that happens, everybody goes down together. Pilot and crew, the expense-account crowd in the first-class compartment and the ordinary folk in economy class.

Something of the same sort is happening to American society as the normal aspiration for a better life comes into direct conflict with the reality of inflation and a slow-growth economy.

What we are beginning to see — in strikes by police and firemen, in the populist uprising against tax loopholes for the wealthy, the general crumbling of the sense of community — is a revolution of disappointed expectations. Unless we either rediscover the secret of vigorous economic growth or come to terms with a world in which overall living standards go down every year

219

instead of up, it is hard to see how American democracy can avoid structural failure.

Governor Brown probably spoke for most people when, in reaction to the strike by San Francisco policemen, he called it "outrageous that police forces can go out on strike."

The other side of the question was eloquently expressed by a striking policeman, earning less than $17,000 a year, who told *Times* writer Bill Boyarsky that the cops didn't want to abandon their beats. But, he grumbled, "A [city] plumber makes $25,000 a year, and a plumber doesn't have to wear a bulletproof vest."

The cop might have added, with even greater logic, that if it's okay for doctors to go out on strike, as they have lately, why shouldn't a policeman or fireman do the same?

It is a fact that the growing appetites of municipal employees' unions were a major factor in bringing New York City to the edge of bankruptcy, and that if elected officials continue to allow themselves to be bullied by these powerful unions, other cities may not be far behind.

If we are honest with ourselves, however, we have to admit that the municipal unions are merely doing what a lot of other people have been doing for a long time: exploiting their positions of power to feather their own nests at the expense of society at large.

Politicians like to talk about public service. But members of the Democratic-run Congress, already earning more than three times the median family income, voted themselves a pay raise just before taking off on their fifth vacation of the year. President Ford, who had proposed a freeze on pay for federal civil servants and military personnel, signed the measure with nary a whimper.

Judge Shirley M. Hufstedler of Los Angeles, commenting on the high attorney fees which prevail these days, observed recently that, "A regular civil trial today . . . is beyond the economic reach of all except the rich, the nearly rich or the person seriously injured by a well-insured defendant."

The answer to such a situation is surely more attorneys, and they are coming out of the law schools in droves. But the legal profession, anxious to prevent a competitive erosion of the fee structure, is said to be in search of a way to restrict the flow of new graduates, just as the medical profession did in years past.

According to Business Week, corporate chiefs enjoyed an average gain of 9.2 percent in compensation in 1974, a year when the average wage and salary earner had to settle for less.

So what else is new? the cynic may ask. Where is the man who, having the power to give himself a raise or to use the power of his union or profession to get it for him, won't do so? It has ever been thus.

True. But people had a mutual tolerance for each other's self-aggrandizement in an era of economic growth, when one man's gain didn't seem to mean another man's loss. Everybody could have a little more each year because the pie kept getting bigger.

For a variety of reasons, that hasn't been happening lately. The purchasing power of the average American's take-home pay is less now than three years ago, and economists can offer small hope that things are going to improve much for years to come.

In practical terms this means that Mr. Blanding can't afford to buy his dream house. His son, the first in the family ever to attend college, finds that a degree is no longer a passport to the good life. His nephew, a high-school dropout with no special skills, faces a future lying somewhere between dismal and hopeless.

It is fine for social theoreticians to say that a lowering of expectations must come. That we live on a planet with finite resources and hundreds of millions of people who live on the knife-edge of starvation, and in these circumstances salvation must come not from endless economic growth but redistribution of income.

But people do not lightly abandon their dreams of a better life for themselves and their children, whether they sweep streets or teach in a university. So the pushing and shoving has begun, as everybody tries to protect his own share of the American dream, and the devil with everybody else.

It is not a pretty picture.

The greatest hope, one suspects, is to rediscover the secret of solid, sustained economic growth—the lubricant without which Americans would not have enjoyed a liberal and humane democracy as long as they have—but this time within the framework of environmental and other restraints.

So far, economists don't seem to know how, or even whether, this can be done. But difficult as it may be, it is a lot more likely to happen than a conversion of the American people into one big tribe of Potlatch Indians, insisting that the other fellow needs all those goodies more than we do. [From Ernest Conine, *Los Angeles Times,* August 29, 1975. Copyright 1975, *Los Angeles Times.* Reprinted by permission.]

C. Construct three effective opening sentences for each of the following topics. Use any of the methods illustrated on pages 212–14 or any of your own inventions.

1. consumer protection in a world of industrial giants

   a. _____

   _____

   b. _____

   _____

   c. _____

   _____

2. the nuclear family—a fading relic?

   a. _____

   _____

b. _____

_____

c. _____

_____

3. the Women's Liberation movement

a. _____

_____

b. _____

_____

c. _____

_____

D. Find three examples of good concluding sentences in recent magazine or newspaper articles, and write them in the appropriate spaces below. Be prepared to tell why you think the conclusion is successful.

1. SUBJECT MATTER _____

   Concluding Sentence _____

   _____

   _____

2. SUBJECT MATTER _____

   Concluding Sentence _____

   _____

   _____

3. SUBJECT MATTER _____

   Concluding Sentence _____

   _____

   _____

E. Revise the draft of the paper you prepared for Exercise 22A or 22B.

8. PREPARING THE FINAL COPY

If you can type, type your final copy on $8\frac{1}{2}$ x 11-inch unlined white paper. Double space so that your instructor can insert comments between the lines when necessary. Double spacing also makes for easier reading. If you must write your final copy, use ink and write on only one side of the paper. The other side may be required for later revisions when your theme is returned to you. Next, space the body of your composition evenly on the page with suitable margins on each side and at the top and bottom. Center your title and place it a few spaces above the first sentence of your text. Capitalize the first word and all other words in the title except articles and short prepositions. Number your pages and endorse your paper in the manner prescribed by your instructor. The endorsement usually includes your name, the title of your paper, and the date.

Before submitting your final copy, read it aloud to yourself (or to a friend) once more to catch any omission of words or punctuation errors. Examine your title in this reading also. Is it brief, accurate, and consistent with the tone of the paper? Will it catch a reader's attention, stimulate his interest? Remember that the title is not part of the composition itself. As mentioned earlier, the first sentence of the theme should not depend on the title for its meaning.

EXERCISE 24

A. Turn in a final copy of the theme you revised for Exercise 23E.

SUMMARY

Like the paragraph, the theme requires careful attention to unity, development, coherence, and emphasis. Because of its increased length and complexity, however, you must plan its construction in greather detail. To help you with this planning, we have suggested the following steps:

1. Decide on a subject. If you can choose the topic, select one from your own experience — one that will appeal to your reader.

2. Limit your topic in accordance with the length of your paper and the interests and background of your reader.

3. Think through your subject.

4. Gather and organize your material; group major and minor ideas, and arrange them in a logical sequence to effect your purpose.

5. Outline your theme. For a short paper, especially one written in class, a rough outline will suffice. For a longer paper the formal outline is almost essential.

6. Write your first draft as rapidly as possible, using your outline as a guide. Put the first draft aside for a few hours, and do not think about it.

7. After you have been away from your first draft for awhile, revise it, giving close scrutiny to content and organization as well as to mechanics. In particular, check opening and closing sentences and the continuity of thought between paragraphs.

8. Prepare a final copy, observing the conventions for preparing a manuscript prescribed by your instructor.

As we stressed at the beginning of this chapter, no simple rules will enable you to write clear, convincing, interesting themes. But careful planning and use of these suggestions in your writing and rewriting will do much to improve your skill and success.

A
B 7
C 8
D 9
E 0
F 1
G 2
H 3
I 4
J 5